Olaf Kaltmeier, Mirko Petersen, Wilfried Raussert, Julia Roth (Eds.)

Cherishing the Past, Envisioning the Future

Entangled Practices of Heritage and Utopia in the Americas

T0308379

INTER-AMERICAN STUDIES
Cultures – Societies – History

ESTUDIOS INTERAMERICANOS
Culturas – Sociedades – Historia

Volume 24

Olaf Kaltmeier, Mirko Petersen,
Wilfried Raussert, Julia Roth (Eds.)

Cherishing the Past,
Envisioning the Future

Entangled Practices of Heritage and Utopia
in the Americas

ШɯЫ Wissenschaftlicher Verlag Trier

Copublished by
UNO University of New Orleans Press

Cherishing the Past, Envisioning the Future.
Entangled Practices of Heritage and Utopia in the Americas /
Ed. by Olaf Kaltmeier, Mirko Petersen, Wilfried Raussert, Julia Roth. –
(Inter-American Studies | Estudios Interamericanos; 24)
Trier: WVT Wissenschaftlicher Verlag Trier, 2021
    ISBN 978-3-86821-804-6
New Orleans, LA : University of New Orleans Press, 2021
    ISBN 978-1-60801-206-0

SPONSORED BY THE
Federal Ministry
of Education
and Research

The project, on which this book is based, has been funded by the German Federal Ministry of Education and Research (Bundesministerium für Bildung und Forschung, BMBF). The responsibility for the content of this publication lies with the author.

Cover Image: Christopher Columbus Statue Torn Down
at Minnesota State Capitol, June 10, 2020

Cover Design: Brigitta Disseldorf

Library of Congress Cataloging-in-Publication Data
Names: Kaltmeier, Olaf, 1970- editor. | Petersen, Mirko, editor. |
    Raussert, Wilfried, editor. | Roth, Julia, editor.
Title: Cherishing the past, envisioning the future : entangled practices of
    heritage and utopia in the Americas / Olaf Kaltmeier, Mirko Petersen,
    Wilfried Raussert, Julia Roth (eds.).
Description: Trier : Wissenschaftlicher Verlag Trier ; New Orleans :
    University of New Orleans Press, 2021. | Series: Inter-American studies:
    cultures - societies - history = Estudios interamericanos: cultures -
    sociedades - historia ; volume 24 | Includes bibliographical references.
Identifiers: LCCN 2020044372 | ISBN 9781608012060 (paperback)
Subjects: LCSH: Collective memory--America. | Cultural property--Social
    aspects--America. | Utopias--America. | Time perspective. |
    America--Civilization. | America--Colonization.
Classification: LCC E20 .C44 2021 | DDC 970--dc23
LC record available at https://lccn.loc.gov/2020044372

Publisher: WVT Wissenschaftlicher Verlag Trier, Postfach 4005, D-54230 Trier,
Bergstraße 27, D-54295 Trier, Tel. 0049 651 41503, Fax 41504, www.wvttrier.de, wvt@wvttrier.de

Copublisher: University of New Orleans Press, 2000 Lakeshore Drive, Earl K. Long Library,
Room 221, New Orleans, LA 70148, United States, 504-280-7457, unopress.org

Contents

Introduction: Cherishing the Past, Envisioning the Future.
Entangled Practices of Heritage and Utopia in the Americas
Olaf Kaltmeier, Mirko Petersen, Wilfried Raussert,
Julia Roth 1

Whither Modernity?
Latin America, an "Entanglement of Spaces"
Javier Sanjinés 13

Memories of Slavery in France and its French
Afro-Antillean Diaspora: Overview of Sites of Memory
and their Entanglements with British and U.S.-American
Images of Slavery and Debates on Reparations
Ulrike Schmieder 31

Envisioning Freedom Futures: Ernst Bloch's *not yet*
and Early Eighteenth-Century Slave Societies
in the Danish West Indies and Dutch Suriname
Heike Raphael-Hernandez 59

The Link of a Former British Prime Minister's Ancestor
to Caribbean Slavery Economy in the Current Call
for Reparations in Jamaica
Claudia Rauhut 77

Memories in Displacement in the Public Space.
The Monuments of Juana Azurduy and Christopher Columbus
in Argentina
Carolina Crespo 101

Populism and the Imagination of the Past and Future

Paula Diehl 123

In the Shadow of Tomorrow: Biological Entanglements,
Genetic Editing, and a New Techno-Utopia in the Americas

Rüdiger Kunow 141

Contributors 159

Introduction: Cherishing the Past, Envisioning the Future. Entangled Practices of Heritage and Utopia in the Americas

OLAF KALTMEIER, MIRKO PETERSEN, WILFRIED RAUSSERT, JULIA ROTH

Abstract

In the introduction to this edited volume, we reflect on heritage, utopia, and questions of temporality in light of recent changes in the Americas, that is to say the rise to power of several right-wing governments. We argue that the focus of analysis should not simply be on changes of government, but rather on long-term transformations which have an impact of temporal imaginaries in the hemisphere. Finally, we present the contributions to this volume.

Heritage and Utopia

The objective of this edited volume is to shed light on questions of temporality in the Americas. In this regard, "heritage" and "utopia" are key terms used to explore the cultural, social, historical, and political entanglements within the Americas and their relation to coloniality, modernity, and contemporary neoliberal globalization.

The last decades have witnessed a heritage boom. The concept can be found in a variety of different contexts (for Latin America, see Kaltmeier and Rufer 2016; for music heritage in the Americas, see Raussert 2021a). Heritage has played a central role for the politics of memory (da Silva Catela and Foley 2019), production of knowledge, standardization of language, establishment of power and hierarchy, distribution of land and urban space, identity politics, and the conceptualization of time (e.g., Western, indigenous, African). Heritage politics dictate social and cultural norms, shape the development of urban and natural environment, and define and re-define narratives of memory and history.

Utopia is a key trope for the very imagination of "America/América"[1] and supported both foundational narratives and independence movements in the Americas. Anibal Quijano and Immanuel Wallerstein differentiate the utopian foundation of the Americas by emphasizing the differences that lie within utopian conceptualizations: North America's "utopia of social equality and liberty" and Latin America's indigenous "utopia of reciprocity, solidarity, and direct democracy" (Quijano and Wallerstein 1992, 556-557). Utopia is at the base of national, transnational, Pan-American, and imperial visions. It formed the base for Barack Obama's promotion of new pluralist cosmopolitan imaginaries in the United States and pro-pelled Evo Morales's push for an indigenous multicultural vision of society in Bolivia. Utopia looms large behind Justin Trudeau's government of diversity in Canada and has continued to nourish protest, resistance, and dissident attitudes toward the social, along with the creation of alternative communal forms. Utopian visions spurred the Zapatista movement in Mexico and the Occupy Movement in the U.S, as well as the current Black Lives Matter movement.

Questions of Temporality in the Light of Recent Changes in the Americas

Recent changes in the Americas have triggered new debates on temporality. The progressive cycle linked to governments like the ones of Barack Obama in the United States, Néstor Kirchner and Cristina Fernández de Kirchner in Argentina, Lula da Silva and Dilma Rousseff in Brazil, and Rafael Correa in Ecuador has come to an end; other governments of the so-called pink tide in Latin America, like the one of Nicolás Maduro in Venezuela, are only a shadow of what they used to be. A new shift to the right goes along with a longing

---

1   On the term "America," cf. Rinke 2019; on the gender dimension of the term, cf. Roth 2014.

for an alleged golden past which has been lost – here we can think about Donald Trump's slogan "Make America Great Again" or Jair Bolsonaros glorification of the Brazilian military dictatorship (1964-1985). In his last book, the late Zygmunt Bauman (2017) refers to this longing as "retrotopia," the return to the past as a vision for the future. But of course, not every struggle for a certain heritage is regressive nor is every vision of the future progressive, as the contributions to this edited volume demonstrate. The call for reparations in Jamaica discussed by Claudia Rauhut and the new techno-utopia described by Rüdiger Kunow are two examples which contradict such a simplified assumption.

Although the recent rise to power of right-wing governments in the Americas is important in itself, we should not just think about it as simple change of government. It rather hints at more drastic long-term changes, especially in regard to the question of temporality. In the age of development, the temporal horizon of expectation was directed towards a foreseeable future. The so-called less – or worse – underdeveloped societies needed to be guided to follow the path of development. The aim of development was to reach the level of complexity or the level of capital accumulation of modern Western societies. Walt W. Rostow explained this idea best in the metaphor of an airplane's take-off. Once the take-off is initiated, here the less developed societies, it will reach the level of mass consumption. In a similar vein, socialist societies promised a societal development through state-run industrialization culminating in the utopia of the class-less society. With the collapse of state-run socialism and the rise of neoliberalism, the promise of development vanished. Francis Fukuyama declared the end of history in global neoliberalism, betraying the liberal ideas of liberty, equality, and fraternity. Nevertheless, Fukuyama was not correct. There is no end of history, instead we are witnessing a certain crisis of the future that relates to the end of great narratives of development and progress. However, this does not mean history has come to an end. On the contrary, the omnipresence of cultural heritage projects, policies of memory, nostalgia, 'retro' and vintage fashion trends, as well as historical shows indicates not the end of history but rather a supersaturation of history in contemporary life.

In the Latin American context, we are witnesses to a real struggle over heritage and interpretations of history. After the neoliberal wave of social, political, and economic transformations of Latin American societies, we notice a massive process of deconstruction of modernity. In the face of economic crisis, we confirm a pulverizing of the social structure that led to the crisis of the middle classes. The social imaginary of progress and development, as framed by Western standards, was hereby dissolved. In the current debate on modernity's heritage, the latter is often discussed under the concept of 'ruins' (Stoler 2003). An emblematic aspect may be the 'self-museumization' of the Latin American capital of modernity, the city that was shaped in the form of an airplane, Brasilia. After only 27 years since its construction, the capital of Brazil has the reputation of being the only city in the world built during the twentieth century to have been granted the rank of Historical and Cultural Heritage of Humanity by UNESCO in 1987.

Nevertheless, most of the heritage debate in Latin America circles around a deeper temporal layer – coloniality. Coloniality is understood not as a historical or aesthetic (in terms of colonial art or architecture) age, but as a long duration temporal layer that is re-interpreted, re-semanticized, and re-used under different contexts and whose repercussions continue until today. In a retro-colonial manner, colonial aesthetics are white-washed from their historical meaning and commodified. This cultural dynamic goes hand in hand with general and profound reconfiguration of society that can be understood in terms of refeudalization (Neckel 2010; Kaltmeier 2019a, 2019b). Taking into account the crescent social polarization and the formation of a global money aristocracy, the demonstrative luxury consumption, the return of walls in diverse spatial units, and the reification of monetary power in political power lead to social patterns that are more similar to feudal societies than to modern-democratic ones. Several elements of these processes can be identified in the recent right-wing governments in the Americas, where the billionaires

Donald Trump, Maurico Macri, and Sebastián Piñeira have been elected president. These processes indicate that history cannot only be thought of in terms of progress and development, nor in terms of post-modernity, but also as a "re-" or a regress to older patterns in new historical situations. These tendencies are probably best expressed in apocalyptic movies that rely on re-feudalized film settings.

In this context, it seems, there is no space for large-scale utopia. But there are fissures, cracks, and niches for small-scale utopias (in plural). Utopia in recent and contemporary times is frequently performative, self-reflexive, and aware of its imperfection. Nonetheless, it continues to inspire artistic, social, and political activism as a trope of change and improvement. Fernando Coronil observed that "carried along by winds of history that fan old flames and rouse new struggles, Latin America has become a diverse fabric of collective utopian dreams," linking these to the negotiation of temporalities: "the dialogue between past and future informing current struggle has [...] challenged place-bound, parochial conceptions of universality and has generated global exchanges about reimagined worlds [...] [that] now unite South and North" (2011, 263-264). However, Coronil warned of the risk that these "new imaginings may be co-opted or crushed" (2011, 263), given the unequal power structures within which these phenomena occurred. This new North-South coalition fueled the protests in Seattle, calling both the People's Global Assembly and the World Social Forum to join for the struggle against neoliberal capitalist exploitation (McKee 2017, 50-51). While the Haitian Revolution, the Mexican Revolution, and the Cuban Revolution certainly remain strong key markers of utopia and resistance having emerged from the South, the Black Power Movement and the current Black Lives Matter Movement provide examples of utopian visions traversing the Americas from North to South.

Radical art practice in the twentieth and twenty-first century shows a strong inter-American imaginary at its base. The Zapatista movement from Chiapas in Mexico has fed in numerous ways the

vision of art and activist practices connecting multiple public spaces
on a local and global level. They were one of the first social movements claiming presence on the internet propagating networks of
'convivencia,' solidarity, and communication, bringing together
radical activists from the North and the South. The Zapatista movement managed to bring The Third World Network from the Global
South into dialogue with radical thinkers from labor activism, progressive ecologism, and solidarity movements from the North. The
imaginaries created by the Zapatista movement, with a unique mix
of surrealist poetics and politics, have traveled far and continue to
provide fuel for grassroots visions of community-building and resistance against corruption and oppressive structures around the
world. Many rich conjunctions of public art and the politics of democracy emerged in the period from the late 1980s with the fall of
the social welfare state to the late 1990s. The Zapatista movement
inspired major movements in the North against neoliberal politics of
exploitation. A major watershed event occurred right at the turn of
the new millennium in 1999. The Battle of Seattle highlighted the
friction underneath contemporary capitalism on the level of trade
policy and global economy (McKee 2017, 53).

The Battle of Seattle also showed inter-American imaginaries at
work in the actions to think of the public sphere and the role of radical art anew. From the Zapatista Revolution to The Battle of Seattle
and the "Carnival Against Capital" in Quebec City during April
2001, imaginaries from the Global South fed the protest movements
in the Northern hemisphere of the Americas. At the turn to the new
millennium, puppetry and street theater were brought to Seattle by a
group that would prove crucial to the Seattle project. A network of
anarchist artists extending along the West coast from the United
States to Canada, the group Art and Revolution represented a major
force to weave together various direct action-oriented environmental
groups and various autonomous groups, thus launching the Direct
Action Network.

Artists took the lead for the media networks via Indymedia as
well as the design of the protests. Puppetry took center stage as a

specific form of street theater embracing anti-closure concerning the art world. It rejected the solemnity and elitism of contemporary art and its related art historical self-references and self-reflexivity so often associated with postmodern artistic expression. On the contrary, puppet theatre fostered the dialogue with the audience, encouraged direct participation and celebrated the joy of communal artistic endeavors (McKee 2017, 56).

Seattle turned out a showcase for the multifaceted ways of art to claim public spaces at the intersection of political, environmentalist, and artist engagement (Raussert 2021b). The actions and performances in Seattle presented a new horizon of a mix of aesthetics and politics. A mix of carnivalesque puppet theatre, banners, and costumes, Indymedia's self-organized public sphere, the action logics of internet shutdown, and Yes Men's cyber inventions created an artistically based movement against neoliberal governance, Wall Street, The World Bank, and similar institutions.

Spectacular performances by artists like Coco Fusco, Guillermo Gómez-Peña, and Kendrick Lamar revisit utopia in performative contexts. Lamar's 2016 Grammy ceremony performance presented musicians performing from within a cage and in chain gang arrangement, symbolizing African American confinement in contemporary U.S. prison settings and linking contemporary injustice to the burden of colonial history. Lamar's performance interpreted the grid as a fundamental 'American' structure – as a "space of entanglement" that sets spatial limits to utopia but also provides open spaces between the metal, steel, and iron through which the voices of the marginalized and dispossessed can pass. These spaces also allow new forms of participation, interaction, and community to emerge that desire new critical utopias by rethinking the social within and against the grid (Raussert 2021b).

The Contributions to this Volume

The authors of this volume explore utopia and heritage, also in their own interrelation, as engines that propel development and change as well as cement hegemonies and hierarchies.

"Aren't we facing a historical impasse because we have no map to determine which routes to the future might work?" asks Javier Sanjinés (University of Michigan) in his contribution, especially reflecting upon the current situation in Latin America. Sanjinés highlights the connection between modernity and coloniality with regard to perceptions of time in Latin America, grounding his arguments in decolonial thinking. He advocates for the use of the essay as a way of tackling the myth of "scientificity" inherent in modernity. Following Sanjinés, the essay could work as a counter-memory linked to movements that operate outside Europeanizing historicism.

An often neglected part of the European legacy in the Americas is slavery. In this edited volume, three contributions, from Ulrike Schmieder, Heike Raphael-Hernandez, and Claudia Rauhut, focus on this topic in different ways. Ulrike Schmieder (University of Hanover) argues in her text on memories of slavery in France and the French Afro-Antillean diaspora that the discussions on memorial sites cannot be separated from the debates on the heritage of slavery and reparations. Based on interviews and archive material, she describes the less well-known case of the Afro-Antilleans in France who have tried to emancipate from the dominating discourse on slavery and white cultural hegemony. She also touches on the entanglements between the Afro-Antillean struggle in France and the debates on slavery in the Anglophone world.

In her contribution, Heike Raphael-Hernandez (University of Würzburg) sheds light on a novel topic in colonial history. She describes the encounters of Moravian missionaries from Saxony with enslaved Africans in the Danish West Indies and Dutch Suriname in the early eighteenth century. Her thesis is that both groups inspired other's political attitudes which were based on a vision of what the German philosopher Ernst Bloch called the *not yet*, a vision of an alternative future. In the case of the Moravians it was the abolition of the German *Ständegesellschaft* and in the case of the enslaved Africans the abolition of slavery.

Claudia Rauhut (Freie Universität Berlin) raises a central question with regards to debates on slavery and to imaginations of temporality in general: "Who can assert, from what position of power and geopolitical knowledge that the past is over?" In her contribution she shows that it is the former British Prime Minister, David Cameron, who tries to close debates about the British colonial past in Jamaica. Debates about reparations for slavery gained new momentum when it was reported that one of his ancestors, General Sir James Duff, received compensation for slaves he owned on a sugar plantation in Jamaica, as well as the fact that Cameron refused to face any debate about this topic during his visit to the island. Rauhut highlights the significance of colonial entanglements between Great Britain and Jamaica and stresses the importance of the current call for reparations for slavery based on media coverage and interviews she conducted in Jamaica.

Debates on heritage can be of profound importance for the imagination of a city and a nation. As Carolina Crespo (University of Buenos Aires) shows in her contribution, public spaces can be the battleground of different ideas of the urban and national heritage. She analyses the case of the replacement of a statue of Christopher Columbus for a statue of Juana Azurday in Buenos Aires. This replacement during the presidency of Cristina Fernández de Kirchner caused a series of controversies around Argentine colonial history and current ethnic identities in the country. As Crespo puts it, the statue of Juana Azurday, although replaced again during the presidency of Mauricio Macri, "expresses the tensions and struggles to challenge the veneration of an urban, national, white, and masculine space, alongside the impossibility of ignoring the role of women and the limits of the rhetoric of indigenous diversity in contexts of neoliberalism."

As Crespo shows for the case of Argentina, the new governments that replaced the governments of the so-called pink tide intend to change the visions of the past and future of the respective nations and of the Americas as a whole. Taking the recent changes in the Americas into consideration, Paula Diehl (University of Kiel), in her contribution, offers a more general political-theoretical insight into the populist imagination of past and future. According to Diehl, populism offers a vision of the future which is very much influenced by the idea of a supposedly lost past. The promise to dissolve the contradictions in modern democracy and to bring the power back to the people is ever-present in populist discourses. Nonetheless, Diehl emphasizes that the relation between populism and democracy is ambivalent. On the one hand, populism can turn into the first step for an authoritarian or even a totalitarian regime; on the other hand, it can also "reinforce democracy by setting free the imagination of the people as the political subject."

In the last contribution to this volume, Rüdiger Kunow (University of Potsdam) introduces a new "techno-utopia" in the Americas to us. His text outlines how the advances in micro-biology and in the biotech sector can change the way people think about life itself. Although the new utopia certainly opens up new possibilities (e.g. to combat diseases), it is also dangerous. As Kunow highlights, the "new utopia [...] is crucially dependent on, and hence deeply entangled in current formations of neoliberal capitalism." Being "genetically at risk" can lead to being part of a new marginalized group in society. Kunow's thought-provoking text, alongside the other contributions to this volume, remind us of the importance of thoroughly taking into consideration the social, political, and economic contexts which are imagined alongside specific ideas of heritage and utopia.

Works Cited

Bauman, Zygmunt. 2017. *Retrotopia*. Cambridge: Polity Press.
Coronil, Fernando. 2011. "The Future in Question: History and Utopia in Latin America (1989-2010)." *Business as Usual. The*

Roots of the Financial Global Meltdown, ed. Craig Calhoun
and Georgi Derluguian, 231-292. New York: New York University Press.

Da Silva Catela, Ludmila and Michael Stewart Foley. 2019.
"Memory politics." *The Routledge Handbook to the History
and Society of the Americas*, ed. Olaf Kaltmeier, Josef Raab,
Michael Stewart Foley, Alice Nash, Stefan Rinke, and Mario
Rufer, 347-354. London, New York: Routledge.

Kaltmeier, Olaf. 2019a. *Refeudalización. Desigualdad social, eco-
nomía y cultura política en América. Latina en el temprano
siglo XXI*. Bielefeld, Guadalajara, San José, Quito, Buenos
Aires: BiUP.

———. 2019b. "Invidious Comparison and the New Global Leisure
Class: On the Refeudalization of Consumption in the Old and
New Gilded Age." *Fiar – forum for inter-american research*
12.1: 29-42.

———, and Mario Rufer, ed. 2016. *Entangled Heritages. Postcolonial Perspectives on the Uses of the Past in Latin America*.
Abingdon, New York: Routledge.

McKee, Yates. 2017. *Strike Art. Contemporary Art and the Post-
Occupy Condition*. New York: Verso.

Neckel, Sighard. 2010. *Refeudalisierung der Ökonomie. Max-Planck-
Institut für Gesellschaftsforschung, MPIfG Working Paper
10/6*. Köln.

Quijano, Anibal, and Immanuel Wallerstein. 1992. "Americanity as
a Concept, or the Americas in the Modern World System." *International Sociological Association* 1.134: 549-557.

Raussert, Wilfried. 2021a. *'What's Going On.' How Music Shapes
the Social*. Trier: WVT, New Orleans: University of New Orleans Press.

———. 2021b. *Off the Grid. Art Practices and Public Space*. Trier:
WVT, New Orleans: University of New Orleans Press.

Rinke, Stefan. 2019. "America." *The Routledge Handbook to the
History and Society of the Americas*, ed. Olaf Kaltmeier, Josef

Raab, Michael Stewart Foley, Alice Nash, Stefan Rinke, and Mario Rufer, 34-39. London, New York: Routledge.

Roth, Julia. 2014. "Decolonizing American Studies: Toward a Politics of Intersectional Entanglements." *Fiar – forum for interamerican research* 7.3: 135-170.

Stoler, Ann Laura. 2013. "'The Rot Remains': From Ruins to Ruination." *Imperial Debris. On Ruins and Ruination*, ed. Ann Laura Stoler, 1-38. Durham: Duke UP.

Suvin, Darko. 1988. *Positions and Presuppositions in Science Fiction*. Kent: Kent State University Press.

Whither Modernity?
Latin America, an "Entanglement of Spaces"

JAVIER SANJINÉS

Abstract

By opening a fissure in the utopian and unquestioned dream of progress, this essay looks critically at the fact that modernity doesn't need to go back to the past except to glorify its own glories, because the idea of modernity is built on the "very modern idea" of its own past. But this past is regional and local – it is European. Reflecting upon Latin America as a "space of entanglements" as well as "entangled temporalities," the essay goes on to question the idea that all pasts that are not European have to be superseded by the march of European modernity and its "horizons of visibility." The essay dismantles this fairy tale, grounding itself in the local history of Latin America. In so doing, it returns to the powerful tradition of the essay as a genre devalued by the myth of "scientificity" inherent to the idea and the fable of modernity.

The editors of this volume have asked me to write an essay on Latin America as a "space of entanglements." Complying with this request, I open my piece with a question rather than an affirmation: Whither modernity? This question will not be answered once and for all, but will be purposely left open. What counts, then, is the set of questions I lay out here, rather than the answers. The answers, of course, should not be dismissed, but should be read as what they are: a series of topics on the avatars of modernity dealing with pressing questions.

Must we always fixate on progress and "building the future," never stopping to consider why we are going through a crisis in the historical project of modernity? Aren't we facing a historical impasse because we have no map to determine which routes to the future might work? Aren't "peripheral" societies – those "spaces of entanglement" that the dominant systems of knowledge have forgotten or left to the dust – precisely the societies that now reject, sometimes violently, the moral and philosophical systems that modernity thought were universal? Doubts seem to have corroded and dissolved every certainty that once shored up our lives and conveniently blinded us so we could go on living in a world that has lost its aim, its sure direction.

What can we do in the face of such pervasive doubt? What holds us in doubt now is not so much the death of the old era as the birth of a new one, an event we can no longer look forward to with the same confidence we had when we waited for modernity to finally arrive. If in the recent past vast groups have found their voice in the key of voicelessness itself, consciousness has arrived uninvited, rejoicing in the empty plenitude of a self, an identity that must still negotiate the thorny pathways that led it to delve into a "ruinous" past, into a "self" that predates the modern self. There, in that space – better yet, in that "space-time of entanglements" – remains today what E.M. Cioran called "the light of pure anteriority" (Cioran 1970, 48). Unable to take refuge in animal howling or mineral senselessness, we humans still find ourselves forced to come up with a new project inspired more by the past and by a constantly expanding continuous present than by a perfectible future. Since I view critically the homogeneous, empty, perfectible future the right promotes, I think it useful to cover some controversial aspects of this goal that we now find dubious. Here, I divide them in three central themes: 1) Modernity in the balance; 2) The conflict over time and the "decolonial turn"; and 3) The essay as a transgressive proposition.

Modernity in the Balance

If modernity is the name of the historical process by which imperial Europe began to build its worldwide hegemony, its mantle of knowledge also covers "coloniality," a set of events that has oppressed vast human groups. Coloniality thus explains the logic that has imposed control, exploitation, and domination on the rest of humankind, which masks this subjugation with the language of salvation, progress, and modernization. If "colonialism" refers to a specific period of imperial domination, "coloniality" is the logical structure of domination that colonialism has imposed since America was "discovered." Coloniality explains the logic of economic, political, and social domination of the whole world, above and beyond the concrete fact that in the past the colonizing country may have been Spain, Britain, or more recently the United States. Therefore, dressed up in "civilization" and "progress," the rhetoric of modernity created an imaginary, a conceptual coherence that derives from the abstract principles of equality and fraternity, as fashioned in the French Revolution. This imaginary generally corresponded to liberalism, the dominant political, economic, and social configuration of the modern world.

However, what modernity leaves out – willfully, it must be said – is any genuine expression of the injustices suffered by the dominated. We therefore think that the colonial experience can only be articulated from the "colonial wound," not from the sensitivities of the imperial victors. Triumphant modernity and its opposite, "modernity/coloniality," are perspectives organized from two different paradigms that intertwine in the colonial matrix of power[2] and that are articulated under structurally heterogeneous histories of language and knowledge. Later in the talk we call this entanglement, after Ernst Bloch, "the non-contemporaneity of the contemporaneous" (Bloch 1991 [1935], 106). In this way, the paradigm of the "dispossessed," those whom Fanon and Sartre termed "the wretched

---

2   The colonial matrix of power should be understood as an enterprise that works on all five levels of human experience: (1) the economic, particularly the expropriation of land, the exploitation of work, and the control of finances; (2) the political, primarily the control of authority; (3) the civic, especially the control of gender and sexuality; (4) the epistemic, that is, the origins and subsequent control of knowledge; and (5) the subjective/personal, that is, the control of subjectivity (cf. Quijano 2001).

of the earth," came about due to the diversity of the noncoeval, structurally heterogeneous histories of those who had to live under the burden of imperial languages and the civilizing process imposed by the lineal and future-directed view of History. This colonial history is what obliges us to distinguish between the colonizer's discourse and the discourse of national resistance. Thus placing yourself within the rhetoric of the French *mission civilisatrice* isn't the same as doing so from the point of view of *négritude* or Indian identity. When we enunciate from the viewpoint of coloniality, we do so from a different consciousness, an alternative consciousness, made invisible by the dominant thought of the West, which Frantz Fanon relates to C.L.R. James, W.E.B. Du Bois, Walter Rodney, Aimé Césaire, and José Carlos Mariátegui. All of these writers, unquestionably metropolitan in their thinking, are "ex-centrics," because their writings purvey space-time entanglements that are distant from and profoundly critical of the prevailing consciousness in Europe and the United States.

The so-called "colonial matrix of power" – of which the Hegelian philosophy of History is a fundamental element – could be observed critically only if a new paradigm were constructed that could understand the difference of the dispossessed, that is, the "colonial difference." As Walter Mignolo rightly observed (2000), this is a remarkably important geopolitical turn within knowledge itself. Thanks to it, we now realize that only when we abandon the pursuit of the progressive development of humanity, can we comprehend that History is a time of entanglements actually interwoven with coloniality in a spatial distribution of nodules that fill a "structural" space. It is even more important to become aware that every historical milestone, in addition to having a structure and not a linear location, is also profoundly heterogeneous. Therefore, if we bear in mind that we are facing not the "end of history," as Francis Fukuyama prematurely declared, but merely the demise of the Hegelian concept of History, we can also comprehend contemporary entanglements as the spatial-temporal intricacies that make up our modernity, fraught with coloniality.

Given that the rectilinear time organized in the West according to abstract universals conflicts with the historical-structural reality of the former colonies, this conflict shows that the differences between our peoples and the Europeans are not merely spatial; they are also temporal. As I argue in my book *Embers of the Past* (2013), Euclides da Cunha, the peerless Brazilian writer of the early twentieth century, observed this historical-structural impasse with particular keenness. And observing it led the author of *Os sertões* (2010 [1902]) to doubt the rectilinear meaning of history. It also caused him to suggest the need for our peoples, who lacked their own histories, to reactivate their memories (of slavery, oppression, racism, marginalization) and to project the embers of the past onto the present. Today, we are experiencing a situation already captured by da Cunha's essay: the philosophy of history has been turned upside down by the growing organization of "societies on the move" (Zibechi 2006). Doubts have also been planted by the increasing self-analysis undertaken by the peoples of the Caribbean and South America – particularly those in the Andean and Amazonian regions – who have been making a troublesome and uncertain "leftward turn."

The Conflict over Time and the "Decolonial Turn"

A keen and level-headed critic of the changing faces of modernity and historical time, the deceased Venezuelan anthropologist Fernando Coronil, argued in one of his last essays (2011) that, after a euphoric embrace of neoliberalism, more than 300 million Latin Americans were ruled by governments that promoted nationalist ideologies associated with socialist principles. While Coronil did not live to see the rather pitiful present situation of the "leftward turn" taken by "madurismo" in Venezuela, "evismo" in Bolivia, and "orteguismo" in Nicaragua, he was careful to point out that, before we ask whether or not the Left has a future, the work of theory is to clarify what notion of the future has led to such a turn, thus constructing what he called rather cautiously the "imaginary future of the present" (232). Regardless of the different and contradictory forms to which this leftward turn gave rise, then, the question is to investigate how the course of history has been reoriented over the past three or four decades.

As we know, the tremor that shook History (once again with a capital H) was less turbulent in some countries and regions of Latin America than in others. The leftward turn in the Southern Cone countries (Argentina, Uruguay, Chile) was basically pragmatic and reformist, eschewing the conflictive revolutionary radicalism that marked the processes that took place in Venezuela, Ecuador, and Bolivia. With actions on the ground, the Andean and Amazonian regions have been only partially successful in shifting beyond the homogenizing idea of a single, universal modernity. We were actually expecting a shift to a "postliberal stage," if by "postliberal" we understand, to put it succinctly, the successful decentering of capitalism on the economic plane, of liberalism on the political plane, and of the nation-state as the matrix that defines social organization. We never expected for capitalism and liberalism to cease to exist; however, we hoped for the significant shift of the discursive and social centrality of these "universal" concepts so that a wide range of social experiences could be considered as possible alternatives.

No matter how painfully inefficient existing revolutionary radicalism has been, there can be no doubt that Latin America has reached an uncertain historical crossroads. Here we see the growth and unfolding of critical theories at least as complex as those that dominated modernity, and richer in every aspect in both advantages and dangers, which point to different trajectories, from Marxist political economy and poststructuralism to what is now called "border thinking and decolonization thinking."[3]

---

3   According to Mignolo, "'border thinking' is precisely what is found in the grumbling of those who have been dispossessed by modernity; those for whom their experiences and their memories correspond to the other half of modernity, that is, to coloniality. It would not be right, indeed it would be dangerous to generalize border thinking and remove it from the historicity from which it has arisen," from the logic of thought historicized in and by "the coloniality of modernity" (2003, 27-28; my translation).

How should a sociocultural challenge as complex and entangled as the one Coronil envisioned be approached? Should this process be examined exclusively from the theoretical space opened up by the social sciences? Wouldn't it be appropriate to involve other forms of knowledge as well, such as the aesthetic forms and concrete experiences of the "lifeworlds" [Lebenswelten] opened up by historical agents that are developing in daily life itself?[4] I believe that questions about aesthetic forms, about the place from which this complex reality should be considered, and about the temporal conditioning that guides our thoughts, are important elements that this investigation must incorporate into our analysis of reality.

Could societies as diverse and regionally complex as those of Latin America – with its indigenous and nonindigenous populations, its individual and collective subjects, living their lives according to both liberal and communal logics – possibly respond to a single, unified historical time? It seems to me that research on time must be particularly sensitive to the fact that we are still living through a conflict that has erupted between liberal modernity, on the one hand, and the communal systems and "alternative modernities," on the other. The conflict between such dissimilar spatial-temporal logics questions today the "leftward turn" taken by our societies. It has given rise to a range of contrasts and entanglements: between neoliberal developmentalist models that are firmly rooted in modernity and anti-neoliberal political movements that have adopted a hybrid modernizing outlook; between the nation-state as conceived under the republic that has been built over the past two centuries, and the experiment – not entirely successful, I must add – of a current Plurinational State; between the national criollo-mestizo culture

---

4   Maurice Merleau-Ponty used Edmund Husserl's term *Lebenswelt* [life-world], a useful neologism that the German phenomenologist coined to designate the worlds – that is, the living contexts, the spaces and times – in which human beings interact and create their intersubjectivity. Concerned with the living present, Merleau-Ponty asserts that "I discover myself in the other, just as I discover consciousness of life in consciousness of death" (1964, 68).

and interculturality; between capitalist development and the socialism that we were attempting to construct and became hard to define;
between the national-popular and the apparently more radical "decolonial turn," also put to question today.

These are sharp contrasts and their novelty is disconcerting.
The background theme, however, is the crisis of modernity. This is a
crisis of discourses, practices, structures, and institutions that are
closely related to the growth of the social sciences and that have
dominated the fields of knowledge over the past two hundred years,
as modernity has clung to the cultural and ontological assumptions
of the dominant European societies. The fact that the dominant form
of imperial modernity has not seduced all European thinkers has also
been crucial. A very important tradition of decentered, "ex-centric"
thinking exists in Europe, devoted to revealing the downfall of the
fictions that we have been living up to now. This is a tradition of
heterodox thought, stripped of illusions, dissenting from the dominant systems, which harasses people of good conscience and confronts them with the necessity of accepting the fall of a civilization
whose universal validity is being questioned. I see a possibility of
engaging a dialogue between this thought, disenchanted with modernity and its idea of progress, and the decolonizing projects we
find in Latin America, particularly those of indigenous intellectuals
who are thinking from their own needs.

I am speaking, then, of the possible formulation of "a paradigm
other,"[5] to be articulated while bearing in mind not only the diversity of colonial histories that are now establishing the "South-South
dialogue" (Latin America, Africa, Asia), but also the outstanding
"place of enunciation" that is Southern and Eastern Europe, which
has been undervalued as much by the geopolitics of knowledge as

---

5   Mignolo refers to this *paradigma otro* ("a paradigm other") as "thinking
     based on and from colonial difference. Not transforming colonial differ-
     ence into an 'object of study,' to be studied from the epistemological
     perspective of modernity, but thinking from the pain of colonial differ-
     ence; from the cries of the subject" (2003, 27). Regarding the "cries of
     the subject," cf. Hans Hinkelammert (1998).

by the philosophy of history derived from Hegel's thought, which promotes progress and development. This decentered Europe occupies an important place in my research, particularly the thinking of those Europeans who question historicism and who, as we will see, have reclaimed an old mission of the essay: to doubt, to meditate, to attain the wise old aspiration of living with dignity, in accordance with nature.

For essayists as diverse, heterodox, and subversive as the Rumanian philosopher E.M. Cioran or the German Jewish intellectual Walter Benjamin (1968 [1940]), whose critical reading of the philosophy of history is fundamental to my work, history is nothing but "an imbalance, a swift, intense dislocation of time itself, a rush towards a future where nothing ever *becomes* again" (Cioran 1983, 33). In his ruthless attack on historical time, Cioran conceives of it as a time so taut that it is hard to see how it won't shatter when it comes into contact with concrete reality.

Is this view too pessimistic? Perhaps, given that it runs a risk of being taken as an apology for irrationality. In the same way that we affirm our need to explore our identity by regressing to an earlier self than the one modernity has constructed for us, we also postulate the existence of "an other" time within historical time – what Bloch referred to as "persistence of 'then' within 'now'" – and we argue that, by introducing the past into the present, this "other time" is incapable of projecting itself "forward," unable to escape into the future, the hereafter.[6] Its disappearance is related to the fact that it is

---

6   In his suggestive essay "Porcelain and Volcano" (1989 [1969]), Gilles Deleuze makes some observations about time that are very much to the point of this strange "hardening" of the present that I am explaining. For Deleuze, "the alcoholic does not live at all in the imperfect or in the future, the alcoholic has only a past perfect. In drunkenness, the alcoholic puts together an imaginary past, as if the softness of the past participle came to be combined with the hardness of the present auxiliary: I have-loved, I have-done, I have-seen … Here the past perfect does not at all express a distance or a completion" (1989, 180). Much like Deleuze's explanation of verbal tenses as used by the alcoholic, Andean subjectivity also seems to cling to the use of this hardened past perfect, which,

impossible to measure social life with the yardstick of the future; the criterion we should follow is that social life belongs to the present because it is always in construction, while the future plays a lesser role.

In his observation on future utopias, Coronil correctly noted a theme that I will now cover as a fundamental element in my own interpretation of contemporary aesthetics: the crisis of historical time and uncertainty about the shape of the future clash with the contents of political activism in the present (2011b), be it on the Right or on the Left. Given that political activism has no given a priori form, being mutable in nature, the heterogeneity of Latin America obliges us to think about reality from different conceptions of history and from a variety of cosmogonies. We must face the fact that our nations contain many nations, that a new diversity of internal communities must give rise to multiple views of the world. Thus, the appearance of "societies on the move" (Zibechi 2006) has placed in the public arena a wide range of social actors and times that overlap each other and give rise to diverse concepts of life.

The seed of doubt planted here about the future is not only the result of the crisis of liberalism and its free-trade practices; it is also linked to the deterioration and disparagement of socialism and its collapse at the end of the twentieth century, a fact that gave rise to the widely trumpeted victory of capitalism and to the so-called "end of History." But the political changes produced by the crisis in the capitalist system, and in particular the controversial leftward turn that Coronil mentioned in his essay, have a clear result: history has not ended. On the contrary, it has returned to haunt us with unprecedented strength. But how should we think of it now? What kind of history governs us? What future inspires it? Is it possible to imagine aesthetic forms that can interpret this new reality?

---

faded and powerless, leaves the future hanging, replacing it with the hardness of this present that is related to the "effect of flight of the past" (1989, 181).

The Essay as a Transgressive Proposition

My aim in this final and longer section is to probe the category and even the status of the "foundational essays" that oriented the construction of the nation-state in the century after independence. It should be taken into account if we are to seek a future, comparing them and questioning them with my version of what the essay could be as a transgressive genre confronting the current rationalizing state of modernization. My version of the essay – a very subjective one, undoubtedly – is tied to the critical processes of the historical time that give the essay its subversive, transgressive function.

Without scorning or underestimating the ability of any genre to subvert reality, I emphasize the role of the essay because I find in it a particularly keen capacity to think in fragments and against the grain of the historical time set up by the totalizing linearity of modernity.[7] The essay, then, is provisional in character, and doubt is its fundamental characteristic. In Latin America, however, there is a close relationship between the essay and the rationalist nature of the nation-building project, with its Enlightenment roots. This close relationship between "literary Americanism" and the European Enlightenment would complicate any possible connection between the essay and the aesthetic representation of decolonization. Aware of this situation, I still think it is worth looking into the relationship between the loss of the unity, the homogeneity, the perfectibility of the historical project of modernity, and my approach to the nature of the essay as an appropriate transgression for uncertain times such as these, with the crisis now developing about the theme of decolonization.

The close relationship between the essay and nation building in Latin America is beyond question. Given the profoundly rationalist

---

7   I am aware of the subversive capacity of other literary genres, especially poetry. José Rabasa has written of the "rage without ends" that Arthur Rimbaud showed in his poetry (2010, 263). Devoted to the repopulation that came about with the Paris Commune, whose struggle to achieve autonomy went well beyond the limits imposed by the state, Rimbaud exemplifies the "poetics of resistance" to the multiple singularities that tried to dismantle it (cf. Rabasa 2010, 138-147).

and historicist nature of the Latin American essay, one has to ask whether it wouldn't be unfruitful to rethink it at a decolonizing moment that is struggling against the current of the Europeanizing project that gave birth to the foundational Latin American essay, as I have briefly argued here. I think there are powerful reasons to reclaim this genre for the needed liberatory ends; to rethink it against the current of the instrumental rationality introduced by modern culture; and to connect it with the conflicts raised by that "other America" about which Edward Said has spoken (2003).

Seen from Europe, which has also had its thinkers in exile, excentric essayists, critics of instrumental reason, the rejection of the Hegelian concept of history as progress, as the identity of subject and object, appears in the construction of history in fragments that was advanced by Adorno, Said, and Benjamin, mainly the two latter, for whom the essay "rubs history against the grain," struggles against the spirit of the era, and, by introducing the "embers of the past" into the present, focuses history backward rather than forward (Benjamin 1968 [1940]). Let me be clear: rather than following European critical thinking as if it were a prescription for today's Latin America, I want to put its reasoning to use in organizing the argument of transgression. We must construct a "border epistemology" (Mignolo 2000) that will let us talk from various systems of knowledge, one of which is European ex-centric critical thought about modernity and its historical time.

To think the local from the past, I believe we should reclaim the essay as the form that makes it possible to question the four rhetorical preconceptions of modernity. The first one is the preconception that the nation is a collective "we" (this common "we" deriving from the imaginary of European history) that can overcome differences by using an all-encompassing rhetoric that pays only lip service to the rightful claims of diversity.

The second relates to the difficulty that the rhetoric of modernity has in accepting the controversial nature of historicism, supporting its homogenizing view with the concept that history obeys "objective" laws. The critique of this view brings us to the basic argument of Adorno (2000 [1958]), who, as Susan Buck-Morss has observed, rejected any "ontological, positive definition of history's philosophical meaning" (1977, 49). There can thus be no "objective" law of history that is independent of human actions and that can guarantee the progress of society.

Without stopping to consider the origin of its enunciation (who speaks and for whom), the historicist project sets up a third stumbling block: its radical intolerance for anyone who dissents from power, conceiving any kind of dissent as a complaint coming from the irrational "anti-nation." In this sense, the dominant narrative declares unacceptable any sort of knowledge that does not come from what has been formulated "from above" by the authorities who hold power. Since the essay is thought of as a counter-memory linked to subaltern groups, to critical collectivities that operate "outside" Europeanizing historicism and from the "outskirts" of modernity, its transgressive role must move beyond the rationalizations of an elitist discourse that ties the nation to power.

By thinking, after Said, more about "beginnings" (in which the past manages things so that it can return to the present, to question it and trouble it) than about "origins" (taken as utopian, as arcadian), the essay distances itself from *poiesis*, the construction of literary images; recall that in *Beginnings: Intention and Method* (1975), Said established, in the best Platonic style, the difference between the essay and literature. The essay is tied to the world of values, while literature is tied to the world of images and the senses – to reinforce a secular mysticism similar to what Said himself developed in the recent past, and what the Peruvian José Carlos Mariátegui before him developed in the early twentieth century (Mariátegui 1971 [1928]). I am thinking, then, of a transgressive essay that, as an aesthetic proposition tied to the world of values, and as an advocate of the self-determination of nations, of peoples, will seek a nonidentity dialectic to mark the struggle of the nation against itself (in reality, its struggle to free itself) in order to gain recognition and respect for its "first nature" as diverse and pluriversal.

But reflecting on the theme of transgression as seen by two thinkers in exile, Benjamin and Said, I ask myself whether the essay can recover what was sacrificed and lost by homogenizing unity. So I opt for the essay as a transgression that can express "the turbulent richness of life." In tension between the lyrical expression of the poetic and the narrative demands of the mundane, the essay is the genre that conveys the lost, strayed, arcane flow of life.

Since empirical daily life thus needs the essay, this genre is an unimpeachably mundane historical experience because it implies an intellectual opening devoted to connecting the formal with the complex folds of life. The historical experience of the essay thus provides for a particularly interesting exploration of topics connected with ex-centric, space-time entanglements such as the everyday experiences of migration and exile. In this way, the essay opens up to the invigorating presence of topics too often made invisible by historicism. This new historical experience presented by the essay would not be exclusively concerned with the "imagined communities" (Benedict Anderson) of the dominant cultures; rather, it should also reclaim alternative communal experiences, that is, the formerly marginalized and little-explored experiences of ethnic groups, as well as the experience of groups in exile, of communities "on the move."

At the end of his introduction to *Reflections on Exile* (2002), Said argues that exile should sharpen our view of things, not keep us bound up in mourning or, even less, in hatred, which corrodes everything. What is forgotten, what is made invisible, should provide new motives to understand that although there is no return to the past that can be brought fully home in the present, the present must necessarily pay attention to the past if it wants to break with what Cioran called "the quietude of Unity" promoted by European historicism and by its most intimate nationalist aspiration: to construct the modern self.

Confined neither to science nor to philosophy, both of which cling to "abstract universals" as their goals, the essay is, as I put it at the beginning of this section, the literary expression best suited to posing doubts and conjectures about the concrete lives of human beings. To keep from turning into an abstract framework for universals disconnected from the life at hand, the essay delves into experience, into perceptible and concrete life. The essay thus captures the uncertain course of that history. So, as Coronil noted, today neither the Right nor the Left can project a clear, sure, epic fate that might express how human beings might adapt to the community and to the universe. With all totalizing possibilities shattered, with any ability to explain the world in which we are living vanished, aesthetics can no longer double for ethics, an ability that, in the Hegelian sense of the term, could have been conferred in better times upon the national epics.

Ever since European conquest and colonization, the elites of Latin America, both Right and Left, have followed the Western guidelines in having an ordering sense of the future. The problem now is that the horizons of expectation have grown murky and unpredictable. Indeed, the arbitration of those who were traditionally prepared to partake of the banquet of modernity, which consigned large groups of people to an uncertain "not yet," postponed the desires of the "noncontemporary" identities that are bursting into history with such force today. These are the huge sectors of postcolonial Latin American society that were forced for centuries to sit in the "waiting room of history" (Chakrabarty 2000, 8-10).

It seems to me that it isn't for the philosophy of history, which is fundamentally teleological and progress-oriented, but rather for what I call the "transgressive" essay, to capture the revolt of these sectors of Latin American society, which up to now have had a past of great economic and political instability, a chronic uncertainty that has deepened the inequality between the modern and the non-modern, between the modern and the anachronistic, and that has given rise to "the non-contemporaneity of the contemporaneous."

Pushed beyond the horizon of expectations promoted by modernity, the future takes on a spectral form, a ghostly appearance that stalks the paths of our lives. What are these specters from the past? They are specters formed by colonialism – events that, despite independence and nearly two hundred years of republican life, continue to influence (and to disturb) our present. Recognizing and overcoming them is the most important task for our decolonizing enterprise. I therefore put forward this new transgressive model of the essay as an aesthetic contribution to decolonization, as an aesthetic practice located at the margins of historical temporality, a practice that embodies the displacement, even the rupture of the time-form, which ought to be dealing with the empirical experience of the modern/colonial world. Decolonizing means reinscribing the suppressed and the ruinous in the present. So reclaiming the essence of the essay means showing how the time-form – historical time; the national epic; the rhetoric linked to modernity – shatters on contact with real life. In other words, I wonder whether it wasn't a peculiarly mestizo-criollo gesture to adopt a modernity that had no notion of the infinite precariousness of the local. Doesn't the imaginary of the dominant intelligentsia clash with the empirical experience of the modern/colonial world, with the place where the subaltern localization of Latin America is inscribed?

Having observed modernity "from the outside," I can vouch for the fact that Western historical time shatters when it meets the life of our peoples. After two long centuries of homogenizing projects, guided by cultural and political elites identified with the Western notion of progress, today's movements appear to be changing the rules of the game, making the entanglements of "the noncontemporaneous" possible in multiple nations whose respective cosmogonies can disrupt the spatial-temporal form of the nation-state. Thus, the "ruins of the past" – I prefer to call them "embers," a means of reinscribing the past (refusing to turn back the clock) in the debate over the new plurinational states – can set the imaginaries of the present afire. The need to reclaim icons of the past is a symptom that reveals our anxiety over learning that the future is uncertain and that we need to make the present more stable. This is why I prefer to talk about "embers" that illuminate our present-day struggles. This is a new image that reveals the presence now of flames that seemed to have been extinguished but can be brought back to life to feed our utopian dreams.

Works Cited

Adorno, Theodor W. 2000. "The Essay as Form." *The Adorno Reader*, ed. Brian O'Connor, 91-111. Oxford: Blackwell. Orig. pub. 1958.

Benjamin, Walter. 1968. "Theses on the Philosophy of History." *Illuminations*. Translated by Harry Zohn, 253-264. New York: Harcourt, Brace, and World. Orig. pub. 1940.

Bloch, Ernst. 1991. *Heritage of Our Times*. Translated by Neville Plaice and Stephen Plaice. Berkeley: University of California Press. Orig. pub. 1935.

Buck-Morss, Susan. 1977. *The Origin of Negative Dialectics: Theodor W. Adorno, Walter Benjamin, and the Frankfurt Institute*. New York: Free Press.

Chakrabarty, Dipesh. 2000. *Provincializing Europe: Postcolonial Thought and Historical Difference*. Princeton, NJ: Princeton University Press.

Cioran, E.M. 1970. "Encounter with the Void." Translated by Frederick Brown. *Hudson Review* 23.1: 37-48.

———. 1983. "After History." *Drawn and Quartered*. Translated by Richard Howard, 33-45. New York: Seaver Books.

Coronil, Fernando. 2011. "The Future in Question: History and Utopia in Latin America (1989-2010)." *Business As Usual: The Roots of the Global Financial Breakdown*, ed. Craig Calhoun and Georgi Derluguian, 231-292. New York: New York University Press/SSRC.

Da Cunha, Euclides. 2010. *Backlands: The Canudos Campaign*. Translation of *Os sertões: Campanha de Canudos*, by Elizabeth Lowe. New York: Penguin. Orig. pub. 1902.

Deleuze, Gilles. 1989. "Porcelain and Volcano." *The Logic of Sense*. Translated by Mark Lester with Charles Stivale, 176-185. New York: Columbia University Press. Orig. pub. 1969.

Hinkelammert, Hans. 1998. *El grito del sujeto*. San José, Costa Rica: DEI.

Mariátegui, José Carlos. 1971. *Seven Interpretive Essays on Peruvian Reality*. Translation of *Siete ensayos de interpretación de la realidad peruana*, by Marjory Urquidi. Austin: University of Texas Press. Orig. pub. 1928.

Merleau-Ponty, Maurice. 1964. *The Primacy of Perception and Other Essays*. Translated by William Cobb. Evanston, IL: Northwestern University Press.

Mignolo, Walter. 2000. *Local Histories/Global Designs: Coloniality, Subaltern Knowledges, and Border Thinking*. Princeton, NJ: Princeton University Press.

———. 2003. "'Un paradigma otro' Colonialidad global, pensamiento fronterizo y cosmopolitismo crítico." Preface to the Spanish translation of *Historias locales/Diseños globales: Colonialidad, conocimientos subalternos y pensamiento fronterizo*. Translated by Juan María Madariaga and Cristina Vega Solís, 19-60. Madrid: Ediciones Akal.

Quijano, Aníbal. 2001. "Colonialidad del poder y clasificación social." *Journal of World-Systems Research* 6.2: 342-386.

Rabasa, José. 2010. *Without History: Subaltern Studies, the Zapatista Insurgency, and the Specter of History*. Pittsburgh: The University of Pittsburgh Press.

Said, Edward. 1975. *Beginnings: Intention and Method*. New York: Basic Books.

———. 2002. *Reflections on Exile and Other Essays*. Cambridge, MA: Harvard University Press, 2002.

———. 2003. "The Other America." Al-Ahram Weekly Online, March 20-26. http://weekly.ahram.org.eg/2003/630/focus.htm.

Sanjinés C., Javier. 2013. *Embers of the Past. Essays in Times of Decolonization*. Durham, NC: Duke University Press.

Zibechi, Raúl. 2006. *Dispersar el poder: Los movimientos como poderes anti-estatales*. Buenos Aires: Tinta Limón.

Memories of Slavery in France and its French Afro-Antillean Diaspora: Overview of Sites of Memory and their Entanglements with British and U.S.-American Images of Slavery and Debates on Reparations[1]

ULRIKE SCHMIEDER

Abstract

The political and social context of memorial sites cannot be separated from the global discussions about the heritage of slavery and reparations. With the increasing visibility of their past, Afro-Antilleans in France emancipate from white cultural hegemony and the dominating discourse on slavery. Although French academic historiography tends to be French-Empire focused in current political debates on memories, connections to the development in the Anglophone world and the agency of international institutions do exist. Because of the hegemony of the U.S. in the media and the lack of French slave narratives, the visual images of slavery in France stem often from U.S. cultural products. The article argues on the base of the documentation of memorial sites and rites, as well as unmarked traces of the slave trade, interviews, archival material, NGO and institutional websites, and current historiography, putting the French case in an Atlantic context.

Until very recent times, mainstream historians like Pierre Nora, the creator of the concept of *lieux de mémoire*, excluded the inhabitants and sites of memory of the Overseas Departments Martinique, Guadeloupe, Guyana, and Réunion from the French nation and its mem-

---

1 Part of my research project on sites of memory of Atlantic slavery in France and Spain, the French Caribbean and Cuba: https://www.hist.uni-hannover.de/de/schmieder/forschungsprojekte/ (cf. Schmieder 2018), funded by the Deutsche Forschungsgemeinschaft (DFG, German Research Fund), project SCHM 1050/5-1.

ories (Nora 1984-1992). But the immigration of Antilleans to the Hexagon makes this approach no longer acceptable. The only prospects for the descendants of the enslaved on the islands who were never compensated for their enslavement are to be badly paid seasonal agricultural laborers on the banana plantations or servants for tourists. After abolition, the plantations remained in the hands of the descendants of slave owners who were indemnified for the loss of their enslaved workers (Oudin-Bastide and Steiner 2015). Unemployment and poverty rates in the French Caribbean are high (Paquet 2009, 89-90) and people are suffering from contamination by the insecticide and pesticide chlordecone (Ferdinand 2015). This is why many Afro-Antilleans leave the island and go to France, about 365,000[2] live there, concentrated in the Ile de France (Abdouni and Fabre 2012). Most of them live in the *banlieue* because nurses and construction workers do not earn wages which would enable them to rent an apartment in central Paris. They brought with them diverse "contre-mémoires" or "mémoires minorées" of slavery (Chivallon 2012, 115-116, 384). The French state and white French society commemorated abolition and silenced slavery and guilt. According to the hegemonic discourse, freedom had been donated by the French Republic to the *affranchis*, who were to be thankful (Cottias 1997).

Commemorations, Monuments, Museums, and Urban Trails in France

In 1998, the French Government celebrated the 150th anniversary of abolition as if the memory of the descendants of the victims and of the perpetrators were the same (*nous sommes tous nés en 1848*) and a war on memories broke out (Coquery-Vidrovitch 2009, 63-84). The confrontations led to the Taubira law (2001, put forward by the Afro-Guyanese Member of Parliament, Christiane Taubira) which

---

2   This number does not include the descendants of the "Domiens" in mainland France.

condemns slavery as a crime against humanity. In 2006, May 10, the day the law was passed, became the National Day of Remembrance of the Slave Trade, Slavery and its Abolitions (Michel 2015, 45-179). In 2017, May 23, the day of the protest march of Afro-Antilleans in 1998, was adopted as National Memorial Day for the Victims of Colonial Slavery.[3] As the emancipation of the enslaved on the islands occurred on different days in 1848, local remembrance days cannot be national ones.[4] The official ceremonies of remembrance on May 10 and 23 take place in Paris, the port towns, and all over mainland and overseas France. They now have become "a month of remembrance" (CNMHE 2017, 2018) and are to be supposed to serve as moral reparation of slavery. So are memorials, monuments, and rooms in museums dedicated to the history of slavery and abolition as well as to white abolitionists and enslaved rebels.

A problem for the practical purposes of commemoration is that in Paris, where most Afro-Antilleans live, there are few traces of the historical slave trade and slavery; where those traces do exist, the percentage of Afro-Caribbean population is not so high. The traces of the slave trade are concentrated in the port towns, the five most important being Nantes, La Rochelle, Bordeaux, Le Havre, and Saint-Malo (Augeron and Caudron 2012, 7). Nantes is the only town

---

3   Proposals to take February 4, 1794, the First Abolition of Slavery, or April 22, 1848, the Second Abolition of Slavery in Paris as Memorial Days were dismissed. According to the historian Marcel Dorigny, then a member of the *Comité pour la Mémoire del Ésclavage*, precursor of the current national committee, a majority had first opted for April 22, a minority for February 4. A storm of protest by the associations (who saw this memorial day as prolongation of "schœlcherisme," the exaggerated honoring of the French abolitionist Victor Schoelcher, responsible for the decree as Under-Secretary in the Ministry of Marine and Colonies), led to the choice of May 10 as a compromise. But the NGO *Comité Marche 1998*, whose president had proposed May 23 from the beginning, was not satisfied with this solution and finally attained its goal, a second Memorial Day (Interview with Marcel Dorigny, May 8, 2018).

4   May 22, Memorial Day in Martinique, May 27, Memorial Day in Guadeloupe, June 10, Memorial Day in French-Guyana.

that allows history to have a very prominent position in the public space, with a big memorial honoring abolition (Vergès 2015) and an urban trail between the History Museum which dedicates three rooms to the topic (Guillet and Gualdé 2009) and the Memorial, going past the luxurious residences of French slave merchants paid for with slave trade money. In Nantes, the Afro-Caribbean community played an important role in the conflicts around the slave trade past of the town, the establishment of the Memorial and other sites of memory, but it is not influential enough to have attained its aims without the support of committed white historians,[5] sympathetic city councilors, and the mayor Jean-Marc Ayrault (Hourcade 2014, 186-228).

The pioneer role of Nantes does not mean that there is no room for criticism. The memorial has little educational value, since a projected connected educational center was not built.[6] Only a timeline of abolitions and a map provide some historical facts. The *Musée d'Histoire* concentrates on slave merchants and the economic entanglements of the town in the slave trade, plantation slavery, and commercial and colonial goods. With some references to mistreat-

---

5	African and Afro-Antillean activists: Peter Lema/*Pasarelle Noire*; Octave Cestor/*association Mémoires d'Outre-Mer*. White supporters: Mayor Jean-Marc Ayrault, Yvon Chotard, Patricia-Beauchamp Afadé, Jean Breteau, *Anneaux de la Mémoire* (responsible for the exhibition 1992-1994 from which the current museum rooms derive), the Museum's director Bertrand Guillet. Serge Daget was the pioneer researcher of the town's involvement in the slave trade (Daget 1975).

6	Interview with Jean Breteau, local historian and member of the association Anneaux de la Mémoire, May 17, 2016. According to him, the monument is closer to the French tradition of the self-styling of the Nation which invented human rights, and less of a critical remembrance of the past. African activists express strong criticisms of this form of memory, as it also has the aim of promoting a positive image of the town in light of its history. They think that this version excludes the African perspective (Hourcade 2014, 223-227), which is really missing. My personal criticism is also that the quotations from laws and speeches about freedom mean little without explanations of the historical context.

ment and the Haitian Revolution, the resistant victim is less present than in Bordeaux's museum.[7]

La Rochelle and Bordeaux have presented the history of the slave trade and slavery mainly in the museums. La Rochelle deals with the topic in the *Musée du Nouveau Monde*. In Bordeaux, a gallery in the *Musée d'Aquitaine* shows the socio-economic history of the town's involvement in the slave trade, ownership of plantations, and enslaved people, particularly on Saint-Domingue, "the Aquitanians' Eldorado," but it also says something about the African roots, the suffering, and agency of the enslaved.[8] There is a big gap between the efforts of the Museum's team and the silence in the rest of the town. The buildings built with slave trade capital (Pétrissans-Cavailles 2004) stay unmarked as such and a small plaque in the area of the port was a pretend-to-remember place until May 10, 2019. That day a more visible statue representing an enslaved woman was unveiled.[9] The docks become a *lieu de mémoire* in Nora's sense every May 10. Saint-Malo sells itself as a *cité corsaire* with monuments or famous *corsaires* like Surcouf and Duguy-Trouin in town, omitting the fact that *corsaires* and slave traders are synonyms. The *Démeure de Corsaire* is in the hands of the descendants of François-Auguste Magon de la Lande, director of the East Indian Company, who admit the involvement of their ancestors in the slave trade only if somebody asks about it.[10] Thus, the hegemonic discourse – Eurocentric, colonialist, racist – on history in the port towns whose wealth was acquired on the backs of enslaved Africans is contested by Afro-descendant associations and sympathizers, but not overturned.

In the white East France, a so-called "Route of the abolitions of slavery" was established with one place dedicated to an enslaved

---

7   My observations, May 18, 2016.

8   My observations, May 10, 2017. Cf Hubert, Block and do Cauna 2010.

9   My observations, May 10, 2019. For details, cf. https://rue89bordeaux.com/2019/05/modeste-testas-bordeaux-rafraichit-memoire-de-lesclavage/.

10   My observations, July 29, 2017, the question was asked by a French visitor.

hero, the Fort Joux in Pontarlier, where Toussaint Louverture died.[11] The other places are dedicated to white abolitionists, but produce very different discourses. In Champagney, the village whose inhabitants demanded the abolition of slavery in the *Cahiers des Doléances*, and Fessenheim, the home village of the family of the famous abolitionist Victor Schœlcher, the sufferings and the resistance of the enslaved do play a role in the exhibition and the guided tour by Serge Robert, *animateur* in Champagney,[12] and Anissa Bouihed, the director of the museum in Fessenheim,[13] respectively. In contrast, Chamblanc with the *Maison familiale* of Anne-Marie Javouhey and an exhibtion hall is a place of hagiography for the gradualist abolitionist Anne-Marie Javouhey, the founder of the order of Saint-Joseph de Cluny, who "prepared" French *engagés* "for freedom" in her settlement of Mana in French Guyana. These Africans found by the French marine on slave trade ships were not immediately freed, but forced to do contract labor. The sisters continue the racist and matriarchal discourse of their doubtful abolitionism of the nineteenth century (Schmieder 2013).[14]

In Paris, the dissonant heritage of slavery has not left as many traces as in London and Lisbon, both imperial capitals and slave trade port towns (Rawley 2003, Castro and Leite 2013). In London, the involvement in slavery is acknowledged in the "London, Sugar and Slavery" gallery in the Docklands Museum (Spence 2011), but not in the public space with the exception of the "Gilt of Cain" Memorial. This monument is hidden away in a courtyard between

---

11 My observations, June 1, 2018. The guide said little about slavery and focused on Toussaint as a military hero.

12 My observations and talk, June 7, 2018.

13 My observations and interview, April 11, 2018.

14 My observations, interview and guided tour, June 10, 2018. The sister who guided me said: "La libération qu'elle a procuré à ces hommes, ça était de leur apprendre à vivre, parce qu'ils vivaient comme des sauvages, ils ne savaient pas vivre en société." Elle = Anne-Marie Javouhey. The sisters wanted to be mentioned as a group, without their personal names.

very high buildings in the city, a historical place of the slave trade business and abolitionist campaigns (Rice 2010, 17-31). Nobody except someone who is searching for the monument would find it there.[15] Plans for a bigger and more visible memorial focusing on the self-emancipation of the enslaved in Hyde Park could not be realized because neither state institutions nor private sponsors were willing to finance it (Dinter 2018, 246-251).

The reforms of Haussmann destroyed most of the residences of absentee plantation owners in Paris, for instance the *Hôtel Massiac* at the *Place de la Victoire*.[16] The Theatre of the Tuileries, where the first abolition of 1794 was promulgated, was destroyed in the nineteenth century. The *Hôtel de la Marine*, the former seat of the Ministry for the Navy and Colonies, responsible for the colonies for good – the abolition of slavery by Victor Schœlcher – and for evil, the repression of rebellions of the enslaved and freedmen, will be the seat of the Foundation for the Remembrance and History of Slavery. This was announced by President Macron during the ceremony marking the 180th anniversary of the second abolition at the *Panthéon* on April 27, 2018. As the French elite does not like to remember the sources of its wealth, the memorial to slavery in the *Jardin du Luxembourg*, near the seat of the Senate, is a small one. It becomes more visible on May 10 when the main ceremony of commemoration takes place there,[17] but on normal days it is easily overlooked. The *association des Amis du Général Alexandre Dumas* led by Claude Ribbe has ensured, with the support of allies in the Paris City Council, that the monument for Thomas Alexandre Dumas, a

---

15   My observations, June 7, 2017.

16   Interview with Marcel Dorigny, May 8, 2018.

17   President Hollande spoke there on the Memorial Days 2013, 2014, 2016 and 2017 (in 2015 he opened the *Mémorial ACTe* in Guadeloupe); in 2018, the speeches were given by Prime Minister Edouard Philippe and the Vice President of the Senate, Philippe Dallier. The absence of President Macron was criticized by committed historians and African and Afro-Antillean organizations. In 2019 President Macron gave the commemorative speech.

Haitian enslaved man who freed himself and became a General in
the French revolutionary army, destroyed by the Nazis, was rebuilt
as a memorial of slave emancipation at the Place Catroux (Dorigny
and Zins 2009, 255).

The Afro-Antillean diaspora was much more successful in the
banlieues than in central Paris. There, sympathetic mayors supported
the establishment of memorials such as the *Gardienne de la Vie* in
Sarcelles in remembrance of the struggle of enslaved mothers for
their children or *Hommage à la Mulâtresse Solitude* in Bagneux, to
honor the female leader of the rebellion against the re-introduction
of slavery in Guadeloupe in 1802. Small monuments to the enslaved
ancestors were set up by the association *Comité Marche 98*, in
Saint-Denis, Sarcelles, Creilh, and Grignet.[18] The association promotes the creation of a big memorial at the Tuileries where all the
names of the freedmen of 1848 will appear.[19] This concept is also
criticized because the names given arbitrarily by state functionaries
to the *affranchis* were not their African or everyday names, many
imposed surnames are even denigrating.[20]

The Influence of Afro-Caribbean Struggles in Great Britain on the French Memorial Landscape

The fight of the French Afro-Antillean diaspora for the recognition
and visibility of the history of the enslaved as an integral part of
French national history through monuments, museums, and new

---

18 Overview: http://www.esclavage-memoire.com/. My observations, May/
June 2018.

19 The idea of the "Mémorial national de la traite négrière et l'esclavage
colonial" is explained on the website of CM98: https://cm98.fr/. The research tool for the names of the affranchis: http://www.anchoukaj.org/.

20 This criticism – that I share – was expressed in interviews with Myriam
Cottias, May 18, 2018, a historian specializing in the transformations in
1848, President of CNMHE 2013-2016, and Florence Alexis, May 28,
2018, curator and *chargée de mission* in the CNMHE until 2017, and in
Chanson 2012, 8.

street names, as well as the removal of monuments honoring enslavers (Hourcade 2014, 179-284; Frith 2015; Dorigny 2017), is a
struggle for emancipation from white-European cultural hegemony;
this is evident as well in the combats of other Afro-Caribbean dias-
poras in Europe. The powerful British Antillean groups have ensured
that monuments like "Pero Bridge," Bristol, and "Captured Africans," Lancaster, have been established, and have thus put an end to
the tradition that only white abolitionists like Wilberforce or Clark-
son were honored (Rice 2010, 24-53). The International Museum of
Slavery in Liverpool (Transatlantic Slavery 2010) and the Atlantic
Gallery of the National Maritime Museum in Greenwich (Hamilton
2007) deal with, amongst other things, topics such as the British
slave trade and the role of port towns and its merchants, plantation
slavery in the British Caribbean, and capital transfer, Black Britons,
and the resistance of the enslaved.[21] The take-off point for many
events and sites of memory was the year 2007, the bicentenary of the
British prohibition of Atlantic slave trade (Paton and Webster 2009,
Tibbles 2008). The new memorial sites coexist with inherited statues
of slave merchants as urban benefactors: e.g. Robert Milligan, William Beckford, and John Cass in London (Dresser 2007) and Edward Colston in Bristol (Dresser 2009, 224) as well as with private
residences and public institutions financed with slave trade capital
(the Guildhall, the Bank of England, the Sir John Cass Faculties and
Schools in London, Queens Square and Theatre Royal in Bristol, the
Town Hall, Royal Institution Building, Blackburne House, and
Bluecoat Hospital and School in Liverpool (Westgaph 2009; Walvin
2011; Donington 2016, 178-181; Dresser 2001, 101-109). Those
places are not marked as slavery heritage in the public space although there are guided tours such as Liverpool's Slavery History
Trail by the black activist Eric Scott Lynch[22] or the Bristol Slave
Trade Trail, promoted by the tourist office.[23]

---

21 My observations, June 10, 2017.
22 https://liverpoolexpress.co.uk/slavery-historian-awarded-citizen-of-
    honour/.
23 https://visitbristol.co.uk/things-to-do/sightseeing-and-tours/audio-tours.

When French communities and state representatives look for
models of the visualization of slavery, they look for instance to the
UK where Afro-Caribbean communities had previously been successful with respect to the establishment of monuments for slavery/
the enslaved and the commemoration of slave trade/slavery/aboli-
tion in museums (Rice 2010, 1-80; Smith et al. 2011). The *Musée
d'Aquitaine* in Bordeaux was inspired by the museums in Liverpool
and Nantes. The idea to include the question of legacies and long-
term consequences of slavery was taken from the British example.
Thus, the Wall of Diversity in the museum of Bordeaux was influenced by the Black Achievers Wall in the International Slavery Museum in Liverpool. Its own contribution was to say more about African and Antillean history from a decentralized viewpoint (Hubert
2012, 593-594). Historical objects presented in French museums
may refer to sources from the British slave trade, such as the famous
engraving of the slave-trade ship Brookes (1789) shown in the
Musée d'Aquitaine.

The symbolic reparations by museums and monuments do not
quiet the debates on material and financial indemnification. French
adherents of reparations of slavery refer to the demands of CARI-
COM, the organization of British Caribbean states, which presses
vigorously for material compensation. Under the presidency of the
Barbadian historian Sir Hilary Beckles, who proved the involvement of many ancestors of current members of the House of Lords
in British plantation slavery (Beckles 2013, 131-142), the Caribbean
reparation commission demands getting back (Beckles 2013, 143-
159, 211-229; Rauhut 2018) the indemnification paid to British slave
owners (Draper 2010). In the preparatory documents for national
hearings on the reparation question of the National Committee for
the Remembrance and History of Slavery (CNMHE) chaired from
2013 to 2016 by Myriam Cottias, I found a reference to this discussion between the UK and its former colonies.[24] The hearings them-

---

24   CNHME, Missions, Décret n° 2009-506 du mai 2009 modifié le 6 mai
     2013, Mandature 204/2016, Archives N° 2, 12 Rencontres citoyennes.
     Auto Saisine: Auditions nationales pour une Ethique de Réparation.

selves never did take place, as the Committee did not obtain the necessary financial support from the Overseas Ministry and there was internal resistance from anti-reparation oriented committee members Fréderic Régent (historian at the Université de Paris 1, the current President of the CNMHE), Emmanuel Gordien (CM98), and Philippe Pichot (*Route des Abolitions*).[25] Former President Hollande considered museums, monuments, and memorial events to be moral reparation for slavery, but refused financial reparations for slavery[26] on several occasions and also to return the indemnification Haitians had to pay for the recognition of independence to compensate slave owners who had to leave the island (Beckles 2013, 206, 213-219; Blancpain 2003). The committee in charge since 2016 is strongly influenced by the NGO CM98 representing French Caribbean and especially Guadeloupean descendants of the enslaved. Its president, Emmanuel Gordien, is a member of the CNMHE. The current president of the CNMHE, Frédéric Régent, appreciates the work of this NGO[27] and participates in its activities, e.g. the march on May 23. The CM98 argues against financial reparations,[28] insisting that the sufferings of the ancestors cannot be re-compensated with money and should not become a commodity. The main aim should be four reconciliations, with "our history, ourselves," with the descendants of the planters, with the French Republic, and with Africa. One step towards that reconciliation will be the remembrance day of May 23 for the victims of colonial slavery. The CM98 collaborates with the

---

25   E-mail-information from Myriam Cottias, August 2, 2018.

26   https://www.liberation.fr/societe/2013/05/10/esclavage-hollande-refuse-toute-reparation-materielle_902048;   http://www.leparisien.fr/politique/-commemorations-de-l-esclavage-hollande-taubira-et-le-reverend-jackson-reunis-10-05-2016-5783833.php.

27   Interview with Frédéric Régent, 9 May 2018.

28   Communiqué de presse. esclavage colonial: non aux réparations financières, 6.5.2013. https://cm98.fr/communique-de-presse/communique-de-presse-esclavage-colonial-non-aux-reparations-financieres/. This position has not changed (Interview with Emmanuel Gordien, May 25, 2018).

békés, the white elite families of Martinique, in the foundation *Esclavage & Reconciliation*.

In the CNMHE, whose members are appointed by the Overseas Minister, the following entities e.g. are not represented: the Martinican NGO *Mouvement International pour les Réparations* which sues the French Republic to get reparations for slavery in the high Court of Fort-de-France; the CRAN (*Conseil Représentatif des Associations Noires*), whose President Georges-Louis Tin argues for reparation (Tin 2013); and the Committee of the 10th of May, a platform of 74 pro-reparation NGOs demanding financial reparation[29] by the descendants of slave merchants and owners and agrarian reform. The CRAN refers on his website to extensive contacts with the Anglophone World, e.g. to the Afro-American political leader Jesse Jackson Jr., also a pro-reparation activist, to CARICOM, and also to the Organization of African Union and South African leaders. CRAN, MIR, and CNR (*Comité National pour les Réparations*) Martinique also participated with CARICOM members and African American reparation activists and NGOs in a Reparations Summit in New York, organized by the Institute of the Black World (Araujo 2018, 170). The idea of a common identity of Africans and Afro-Antilleans/Americans as "Blacks" propagated by the CRAN and the U.S. Black movements is often not shared by French Antillean associations and intellectuals (Blakely 2012). Of the theoretical and literary approaches developed by French Antillean writers, *négritude* (Aimé Césaire, Léon Gantran-Damas), *antillanité* (Edouard Glissant), and *creolité* (Jean Bernabé, Patrick Chamoiseau and Raphaël Confiant), only the first identified strongly with African roots and Blackness (Mudimbe-Boyi 2012).

Besides the political influence of British debates, there is a cultural influence. As slavery in the French islands did not produce classic slave narratives, French memory activists adapt British sources.

---

29   Besides MIR and CRAN, p.e. COFFAD (Collectif des Filles et Fils d'Africains Déportés), CIPN (Comité International des Peuples Noirs) and the Association des Amis du Général Dumas have demanded material reparations, CIPN since 1992 (Gueye 2018).

The actress and activist from Guadeloupe Souria Adèle uses the French version of the narrative of Mary Prince (Ferguson 1997) in a theater piece staged in the *banlieue* and in schools,[30] and has produced a documentary about the research into the traces of Mary Prince in the Caribbean (Descas and Adèle 2014). To describe the influences of British and American literature on writers from the French Caribbean and the diaspora in France, the debates on the reception of Gilroy's concept of the Black Atlantic and postcolonial/diaspora studies, as well as own traditions of postcolonial thought in France would exceed the bounds of this article which concentrates on sites of memory (Gilroy 1993; Gueye 2006; Miller 2008, 327-363; Agudelo et al. 2009; Forsdick and Murphy 2009).

The Influence of U.S. Debates and Media

Given its status as a global power, the political debates in the U.S. are reported worldwide including those on reparations for slavery. The CNMHE looked at debates in the U.S., at Barack Obama's speech on race from 2008,[31] and the writings of journalist and reparation expert Ta-Nehisi Coates (Coates 2014) from the University of Virginia. I found in the archives of the Committee the report of the Durban Conference against Racism of 2001, the ideas of the African Union on transitional justice, and one document on Columbian maroon village rights, but none on other Hispanic American regions and its research boom about "the third root,"[32] the movements of *afrodescendientes,* nor the Spanish-American activities in the International Decade for People of African Descent. There was no document on Brazil, although there is a decade-long discussion in Brazil on reparations of slavery; it produced some success for Afro-

---

30 https://ciemanlala.com/tag/souria-adele/, 21.8.2018.
31 *The New York Times*, 18.3.2008, Barack Obama's Speech on Race, https://www.nytimes.com/2008/03/18/us/politics/18text-obama.html.
32 Overview on bibliography: Andrews 2004, 339-378; Martinez Montiel 2012, 631-650.

Brazilians, affirmative action, e.g. in universities, and access to landownership for the inhabitants of runaway settlements, mostly enshrined in law, but slowly obtained in practice (Araujo 2018, 169-173). African American leaders are invited to the national commemorative ceremony on May 10 to Paris. In 2016, civil rights leader Jesse Jackson and in 2018 a delegation of the National Museum of African American History and Culture participated in the national commemorative event in the *Jardin du Luxembourg*.

For the Afro-Antilleans in the French Caribbean and its diaspora in France, the socio-economic, political, and cultural gains of African Americans, particularly after the election of Barack Obama as President of the United States (Dubois 2019), and the achievements with respect to the remembrance of slavery and past resistance, serve as examples. The National Museum of African American History and Culture in Washington's National Mall and other African American Museums (Eichstedt and Small 2002, 233-256; Burns 2013), monuments such as the Harriet Tubman Memorial in Boston, the Memorial to the Underground Railroad in Detroit, and the Sojourner Truth Memorial in Battle Creek, excavations and presentations of slave quarters (Isaac Royall House in Medford, Chan 2007), or burial grounds (African Burial Ground in New York, Frohne 2015; cemetery of the enslaved at President's House in Philadelphia, Aden 2015), are all examples of what Afro descendants can achieve. The gains serve as an example for Afro-French groups although in the U.S. memorial landscape, particularly in the South, the memories of the slaveholder elite are still more present than the memories of the enslaved and slavery is often neglected and trivialized (Eichstedt and Small 2002, 105-169, 257-270).

Literary and visual representations of Atlantic slavery are strongly marked by the global hegemony of the United States in the book market, film industry, and mass media. TV series and movies like "Roots" (1977), "North and South" (1985-1994), "Glory" (1989), "Amistad" (1997), "Beloved" (1998), "Lincoln" (2012), "Django Unchained" (2012), and "Twelve Years a Slave" (2013) mark the global image of slavery. They do not transmit a common message, since some of them put the lives and resistance of the enslaved at the center of the story, e.g. "Roots," whilst others continue to idealize white abolitionists and put African Americans at the margins, e.g. "Lincoln." Even the racist movie "Gone with the Wind" (1939), which glorifies slaveholding Southerners, defends slavery, and ridicules African Americans, is still regularly shown on TV all over the world.[33]

Until now, U.S. hegemony in the media had the effect of making French people see slavery as it was portrayed in U.S.-American films and series. Some efforts were made to overcome this with TV series and films on the slave trade, slavery, and abolition in the French Antilles *Rue Cases-Nègres* (1983), *Sucre Amer* (1998), *Le Passage du Milieu* (2001), *1802 l'épopée guadeloupéenne* (2005), *Tropiques amers* (2006), *Case Départ* (2010), or the four part documentary *Les routes de l'esclavage* shown in May 2018 on France Ô and ARTE. The TV series *Tropiques amers* supervised by expert on slavery history Myriam Cottias, excellently informed about what historians found out about slavery and social relations, focusing on the enslaved and their agency. Although four million people saw it on France 3, the TV channel did not finance a follow-up (Le Parisien, 17.02.2014). Generally, French black actors are less present in French films and TV than black actors in U.S.-American films and TV (Dubois 2019). The TV programme France Ô (for "Outremer") shows more films and series about the history of slavery than the other French channels, but most of them still stem from U.S. TV and cinema. All movies and series about slavery have a limit: labor and death in the fields play a minor role. Nobody would watch a film showing only deadly daily work, torture, starvation, and death of the enslaved before they were able to have children, the fate of most Africans brought to the Caribbean. The worst of plantation slavery cannot be staged.

---

33   The most recent date on German TV was 5/01/2018 on ARTE (https://www.wunschliste.de/spielfilm/vom-winde-verweht/tv).

Educational material is also often based on sources relating to
U.S. slavery or British Caribbean slavery. The "site pédagogique
EURESCL" is a European Union project made by French, British,
Haitian, and Senegalese teachers and researchers. It helps to teach
the topics of the slave trade, slavery and abolition, and quotes Sol-
omon Northrup, Olaudah Equiano, Frederick Douglass, and Mary
Prince, translated to French (Dossier 2014). This deficit is due to the
non-existence of classic slave narratives, but may change with the
publication of French sources such as the petitions and lawsuits initiated by the enslaved in French colonies (Rogers 2015; Oudin-
Bastide 2015; Régent et al. 2015).

Why should it be a problem that the political debates on slavery's legacy and the image of slavery are dominated by U.S. discourses and pictures although France had its own plantation slavery
islands? From the standpoint of the comparative history of slavery,
because U.S.-American slavery is important for U.S.-American history, but the U.S. slavery is unimportant from a quantitative perspective in plantation slavery as less than 4% of the enslaved Africans were brought to the U.S. and the former British colonies.[34]
Moreover, U.S. plantation slavery was atypical as it permitted – in
contrast to the Brazilian and Caribbean slaveries and as the only
major American slave society – the reproduction of the enslaved
(Bergad 2007, 96-107). This does not mean, of course, that a man or
woman being sold to the Deep South during the cotton boom, separated from their family, and tortured every day to pick cotton like a
machine did not experience hell on earth (Johnson 2013; Baptist
2014). However, most enslaved Africans arrived at Brazil, Barbados
and Jamaica, Saint-Domingue, or Cuba very young and died some
years later of exhaustion after 20 hour workdays during the sugar
harvest. The survivors, until emancipation, were a small minority of
the millions of Africans who died without descendants in the Amer-

---

34 Of the approx. 10.7 million enslaved Africans who arrived the Americas,
    about 389,000 (= 3, 63 %) were brought to mainland North America
    (TSTD).

icas. By continuously referring to U.S.-American slavery, we risk forgetting the dead of the Caribbean and Brazilian killing fields.

There is a gap between political debates on commemoration and reparations for slavery in the media, strongly influenced by the North American example, and French research on historical slavery, which is entirely focused on the French colonies.[35] Some specialists have written about entangled slaveries, such as the slave trade from French port towns to Cuba[36] or the role of emigrants from Saint-Domingue in building coffee plantations in the east of Cuba (Yacou 1994), but this knowledge stays confined within the academy. The Spanish publications on capital transfer from Cuban slavery to Britain and France (Bahamonde and Cayuela 1992, Rodrigo y Alharilla 2013) are ignored and comparative studies on slavery and post-emancipation are mostly published outside France.[37] In contrast, the historiography on memories of slavery sometimes adopts a comparative approach, mostly referring to Great Britain as an object of comparison with France (Chivallon 2005, Hourcade 2014).

Evaluating the U.S. influence, I point to the fact that on the one hand the emancipation from the U.S. model is desirable as the above-mentioned differences between the slavery past of the U.S.-South and Caribbean lead to a false image of the French Caribbean past and impede the search for commonalities with Afro-descendants in Spanish America and Brazil, also Catholic postcolonies where Romance languages are spoken and Roman law traditions were imposed. They also distract from Caribbean cross-island cooperation. On the other hand, the status of Afro-Antilleans as citizens of an overseas department, not independent states, brings them in a comparable situation to African Americans as a disadvantaged mi-

---

35 Historiography: Schmieder 2017, 426-436.

36 116 illegal slave trade expeditions of French ships to the Spanish Caribbean, 107 to Cuba, and 9 to Puerto Rico (cf. Daget 1997, 107).

37 Except Yacou 1992. Systematic comparisons: Tomich 2004 (includes a comparison between Cuba and the French Caribbean, particularly Martinique); Schmieder 2017. There are compilations of articles on different Caribbean or world regions, e.g. Cottias 2010.

nority living in the same national state with former slave owners. The political and socio-economic hegemony of the descendants of enslavers explains the seldom broken silence on a possible land reform in favor of the descendants of the enslaved in the French Caribbean and the U.S. The U.S. and the French state support to a certain degree symbolic reparations like the establishment of memorial sites, remembrance days, and ceremonies, re-naming of streets and places, and educational measures, but they resist material reparations and any change of private property rights. This does not mean, of course, that this rejection of material compensation will prevent real reparations forever. Afro-Antilleans and Afro-American people have a long tradition of resistance and their identity is based on that (Araujo 2018, 83-178).

A Prediction of Future Developments

I will venture here to make a prediction. The most probable outcome of the struggle of Afro-Caribbean and African-Americans is that reparations will be paid by European and American taxpayers, which is justifiable given the advantages whites on both sides of the Atlantic derived from the exploitation of enslaved Africans. In the processing industry of colonial goods or in industries whose initial capital stemmed from the slave trade and plantation slavery, Europeans of the lower and middle classes profited from Atlantic Slavery when they found jobs in the production of textiles, tools, and weapons for export to Africa in exchange for enslaved people or directly to the plantation islands. With the expansion of plantation slavery, they got ever cheaper coffee and sugar. And charitable, educational, and cultural institutions in Europe were often financed by profits from the slave trade and slavery.[38]

What is not so justifiable is that the heirs of enslavers will presumably escape any material obligations as they always have. The

---

38   For an overview of the historiography on capital transfer from Atlantic Slavery to Europe, cf. Schmieder 2018.

investigation of the indemnification of British slave owners for instance revealed who profited (Draper 2010),[39] but no British Government has forced the heirs to pay that compensation back. There are inheritors of the enslavers who admit their responsibility, for instance in the U.S. (Ball 1998; DeWolf 2008; Browne 2008; Tracing Centre of the DeWolf family) and the French Caribbean. The *Fondation Esclavage et Réconciliation* under *béké* rule finances commemorative and educational events and projects, but it does so with the aim of appeasing the public and preventing real reparation such as distributing land or repaying the indemnification.

Sources

Interviews with Marcel Dorigny, Myriam Cottias, Florence Alexis, Frédéric Régent, Jean Breteau, Emmanuel Gordien, Serge Robert, Anissa Bouhed, sisters of Sanit-Joseph de Cluny, for details, see footnotes.

Archives

Comité National de la Mémoire et de l'Histoire de l'esclavage (CNMHE), Missions (This part of the Archive was in June 2018 on its way to the *Archives Nationales de la France*, but still to be located in the Ministry of the Interior. I thank Mme. Florence Alexis, *chargée de mission* of the Committee until 2017, who gave me that information, and Mr. Sylvain Manville who was so kind to let me see the documents in his office).

CNHME, Secrétariat Général (In May 2018 this part of the Archive was still to be found in the rooms of the Committee in the Overseas Ministry. I am very grateful to Dr. Frédéric Régent,

---

39   In France, these investigations began recently with the project "REPAIRS, Réparations, compensations et indemnités au titre de l'esclavage (Europe-Amériques-Afrique) (XIXe-XXIe)," https://repairs.hypotheses. org/a-propos.

President of the CNMHE since 2016, who gave me access to these documents).

Works Cited

Abdouni, Saran, and Édouard Fabre. 2012. "365 000 Domiens vivent en métropole." *Insée première* no. 1389. https://www.insee.fr/fr/statistiques/1281122.

Aden, Roger C. 2015. *Upon the Ruins of Liberty. Slavery, the President's House at Independence National Historical Park, and Public Memory*. Philadelphia: Temple University Press.

Agudelo, Carlos, Capucine Boidin, and Livio Sansone, eds. 2009. *Autour de "l'Atlantique noir." Une polyphonie de perspectives*. Paris: Éditions d'IHEAL.

Andrews, George Reid. 2004. *Afro-Latin America, 1800-2000*. Oxford: Oxford University Press.

Araujo, Ana Lucia. 2018. *Reparations for Slavery and the Slave Trade. A Transnational and Comparative History*. London, New York: Bloomsbury Academic.

Augeron, Mickaël, and Olivier Caudron, eds. 2012. *La Rochelle, l'Aunis et la Saintonge face à l'esclavage*. Paris: Les Indes savantes.

Bahamonde, Angel, and José Cayuela. 1992. *Hacer las Américas: las elites españolas en el siglo XIX*. Madrid: Alianza Editorial.

Ball, Edward. 1998. *Slaves in the Family*. London: Penguin Books.

Baptist, Edward E. 2014. *The Half Has Never Been Told: Slavery and the Making of American Capitalism*. New York: Basic Books.

Beckles, Hilary M. 2013. *Britain's Black Debt: Reparation for Caribbean Slavery and Native Genocide*. Kingston: University of the West Indies Press.

Bergad, Laird W. 2007. *The Comparative Histories of Slavery in Brazil, Cuba, and the United States*. Cambridge: Cambridge Universiy Press.

Blakely, Allison. 2012. "Coda: Black Identity in France in a European Perspective." *Black France/France Noire. The History and Politics of Blackness*, ed. Trica Danielle-Keaton, T. Denean Sharpley-Whiting, and Tylor Stovall, 287-305. Durham, London: Duke University Press.

Blancpain, François. 2003. "Note sur les 'dettes' de l'esclavage: le cas de l'indemnité payée par Haïti (1825-1883)." *Outre-mers* 90.340-341: 241-245.

Brown, Katherine. 2008. *Traces of the Trade: A Story from the Deep North*. Documentary Film.

Burns, Andrea A. 2013. *From Storefront to Monument: Tracing the Public History of the Black Museum Movement*. Amherst: University of Massachusetts Press.

Castro Henriques, Isabel, and Pedro Pereira Leite. 2013. *Lisboa, cidade africana. Percursos e lugares de memoria da presença africana*. Lisbon: Marca d'Água.

Chan, Alexandra A. 2007. *Slavery in the Age of Reason: Archaeology at a New England Farm*. Knoxville, TN: University of Tennessee Press.

Chanson, Philippe. 2012. "Du son à l'inscription, la trace indélébile du nom. À propos d'une blessure héritée de l'esclavage aux Antilles-Guyane." *Sens-Dessous* 10: 4-14.

Chivallon, Christine. 2005. "L'usage de la mémoire de l'esclavage dans les anciens ports négriers de Bordeaux et Bristol." *L'esclavage, la colonisation, et après..., France, États-Unis, Grande-Bretagne*, ed. Patrick Weil and Stéphane Dufoix, 559-584. Paris: PUF.

———. 2012. *L'esclavage, du souvenir à la mémoire, Contribution à une anthropologie de la Caraïbe*. Paris: Karthala.

CNHME. 2017. *Journée nationale des Mémoires de la traite, de l'esclavage & de leurs abolitions. Agenda 2017 des Mémoires de la traite, de l'esclavage & de leurs abolitions*. Paris: CNMHE.

———. 2018. *En finir avec les traites et les esclavages*. Paris: CNHME.

Coates, Ta-Nehisi. 2014. "The Case for Reparations." *The Atlantic*, June 2014. https://www.theatlantic.com/magazine/archive/2014/06/the-case-for-reparations/361631/.

Coquéry-Vidrovitch, Cathérine. 2009. *Enjeux politiques de l'histoire coloniale*. Marseille: Agone.

Cottias, Myriam. 1997. "L'oubli du passé contre la citoyenneté: troc et ressentiment à la Martinique (1848-1946)." *1946-1996. Cinquante Ans de Départementalisation Outre-Mer*, ed. Fred Constant and Justin Daniel, 293-313. Paris: L'Harmattan.

———, Élisabeth Cunin, and António de Almeida Mendes, eds. 2010. *Les traites et les esclavages. Perspectives historiques et contemporaines*. Paris: Karthala.

Daget, Serge. 1975. "Long cours et négriers nantais du trafic illégal, 1814-1833." *Outre-mers* 62.226-227: 90-134.

———. 1997. *La répression de la traite des Noirs au XIXe siècle. L'action des croisières françaises sur les côtes occidentales de l'Afrique (1817-1850)*. Paris: Karthala.

Descas, Alex, and Souria Adèle. 2014. *Mary Prince, d'après The History of Prince. Récit autobiographique d'une esclave antillaise*. Paris: Compagnie Man Lala. 2014.

DeWolf, Thomas Norman. 2008. *Inheriting the Trade: A Northern Family Confronts its Legacy as the largest Slave-Trading Dynasty in U.S. History*. Boston: Beacon Press.

Dinter, Sonia. 2018. *Die Macht der historischen Handlung. Sklaverei und Emanzipation in der britischen und französischen Erinnerungskultur seit Ende der 1990er Jahre*. Bielefeld: transcript.

Donington, Katie. 2016. "Local Roots/Global Routes. Slavery, Memory and Identity in Hackney." *Britain's History and Memory of Transatlantic Slavery: Local Nuances of a "National Sin"*, ed. Katie Donington, Ryan Hanley, and Jessica Moody, 172-194. Liverpool: Liverpool University Press.

Dorigny, Marcel. 2018. *Arts & Lettres contre l'esclavage*. Paris: Cercle d'Art.

———. 2017. "A Paris, il faudrait redonner du sens plutôt qu'effacer les noms." *Libération*, 22.8.2017.

————, and Max-Jean Zins, eds. 2009. *Les traites négrières coloniales. Histoire d'un crime.* Paris: Cercle d'Art.

Draper, Nicholas. 2010. *The Price of Emancipation. Slave-Ownership, Compensation, and British Society at the End of Slavery.* Cambridge: Cambridge University Press.

Dresser, Madge. 2009. "Remembering Slavery and Abolition in Bristol." *Slavery and Abolition* 30.2: 223-246.

————. 2007. "Set in Stone? Statues and Slavery in London." *History Workshop Journal* 64.1: 162-199.

————. 2001. *Slavery Obscured: The Social History of the Slave Trade in an English Provincial Port.* London: Continuum.

Dubois, Régis. 2013. "Noirs et Blacks au cinéma: regards croisés France/Etats-Unis." *Le sens des images*, 21.04.2013. http://lesens desimages.com/2013/04/21/noirs-et-blacks-au-cinema-regards--croises-franceetats-unis/.

Eichstedt, Jennifer, and Stephen Small. 2002. *Representations of Slavery. Race and Ideology in Plantation Museums* Washington: Smithsonian Institution.

EURESCL. 2014. *DOSSIER PAROLES D'ESCLAVES.* http://educa tion.eurescl.eu/index.php/fr/2012-08-14-22-01-21/paroles-d-esclaves.

Ferdinand, Malcolm. 2015. "De l'usage du chlordécone en Martinique et en Guadeloupe: l'égalité en question." *Revue française des affaires sociales* 1-2: 163-183.

Ferguson, Moira, ed. 1997. *Mary Prince: The History of Mary Prince: a West Indian Slave, Related by Herself.* Ann Arbor: University of Michigan Press. Orig. pub. 1831.

Forsdick, Charles, and David Murphy. 2009. "Introduction: Situating Francophone Postcolonial Thought." *Postcolonial Thought in the French-speaking World*, ed. Charles Forsdick and David Murphy, 1-27. Liverpool: Liverpool University Press.

Frith, Nicola. 2015. "The Art of Reconciliation: the Memorial to the Abolition of Slavery in Nantes." *At the Limits of Memory: Legacies of Slavery in the Francophone World*, ed. Nicola Frith and Kate Hodgson, 68-89. Liverpool: Liverpool University Press, 2015.

Frohne, Andrea E. 2015. *The African Burial Ground in New York City: Memory, Spirituality, and Space*. Syracuse, NY: Syracuse University Press.

Gallas, Kristin L., and James DeWolf Perry. 2015. *Interpreting Slavery at Museums and Historic Sites*. Lanham, MD: Rowman & Littlefield.

Gilroy, Paul. 1993. *The Black Atlantic: Modernity and Double Consciousness*. Cambridge, Mass.: Harvard University Press.

Gueye, Abdoulaye. 2006. "De la diaspora noire: enseignements du contexte français." *Revue européenne des migrations internationales* 22.1: 11-33.

———. 2018. "The Past is a Contentious Field: The Memory of the Atlantic Slave Trade in the Black Organizational Dynamic." *A Stain on our Past. Slavery and Memory*, ed. Abdoulaye Gueye and Johan Michel, 91-114. Trenton: African World Press.

Guillet, Bertrand, and Krystel Gualdé. *Le Musée d'Histoire de Nantes. Château des Ducs de Bretagne*. Nantes: Musée d'histoire de Nantes, 2009.

Hamilton, Douglas J., and Robert J. Blyth. 2007. *Representing Slavery: Art, Artefacts, and Archives in the Collections of the National Maritime Museum*. Aldershot: Lund Humphries.

Hourcade, Renaud. 2014. *Les ports négriers face à leur histoire: politique de la mémoire à Nantes, Bordeaux et Liverpool*. Paris: Dalloz.

Hubert, François. 2012. "Un exemple de commémoration critique: comment exposer l'esclavage dans un musée grand-public. Le cas du Musée d'Aquitaine." *Outre-mers* 99.376-377: 591-607.

———, Christian Block, and Jacques de Cauna. 2010. *Bordeaux au XVIII siècle. Le commerce atlantique et l'esclavage. Bordeaux in the 18th Century. Transatlantic Trading and Slavery*. Bordeaux: Le Festin.

Johnson, Walter. 2013. *River of Dark Dreams. Slavery and Empire in the Cotton Kingdom*. Cambridge, MA: Belknap Press of Harvard University Press.

Le Parisien. 2014. "L'esclavage, dernier tabou du cinéma français." http://www.leparisien.fr/espace-premium/culture-loisirs/l-esclavage-dernier-tabou-du-cinema-francais-17-02-2014-3597469.php.

Martinez Montiel, Luz María, ed. 2012. *Afroamérica II, Africanos y Afrodescendientes*. Mexico City: UNAM.

Michel, Johann. 2015. *Devenir descendant d'esclave. Enquête sur les régimes mémoriels*. Rennes: Presses Universitaires de Rennes.

Miller, Christopher L. 2008. *The French Atlantic Triangle: Literature and Culture of the Slave Trade*. Durham: Duke University Press.

Mudimbe-Boyi, Elisabeth. 2012. "Black France: Myth or Reality? Problems of Identity and Identification." *Black France/France Noire. The History and Politics of Blackness*, ed. Trica Danielle Keaton, T. Denean Sharpley-Whiting, and Tylor Stovall, 17-31. Durham & London: Duke University Press.

Nora, Pierre. 1984-1992. *Les lieux de mémoire*, t. 1-3.3, Paris: Gallimard.

Oudin-Bastide, Caroline. 2015. *Maîtres accusés, esclaves accusateurs: les procès Gosset et Vivié (Martinique, 1848)*. Mont-Saint-Aignan: Presses universitaires de Rouen et du Havre.

———, and Philippe Steiner. 2015. *Calcul et morale: coûts de l'esclavage et valeur de l'émancipation (XVIIIe-XIXe siècle)*. Paris: Albin Michel.

Paquet, Marc-Emmanuel. 2009. *Regard sur l'économie martiniquaise. Essai*. Fort-de-France: K. Éditions.

Paton, Diana, and Jane Webster, eds. 2009. *Slavery and Abolition* 30.2. "Special Issue: Remembering Slave Trade Abolitions: Reflections on 2007 in International Perspective".

Pétrissans-Cavailles, Danielle. 2004. *Sur les traces de la traite des noirs à Bordeaux*. Paris: L'Harmattan.

Rawley, James. 2003. *London, Metropolis of the Slave Trade.* Columbia: University of Missouri Press.

Rauhut, Claudia. 2018. "Caribbean Leaders in the Transnational Struggle for Slavery Reparations." *Reshaping Glocal Dynamics of the Caribbean: Relaciones y Deconexiones – Relations et Déconnexions – Relations and Disconnections,* ed. Anja Bandau, Anne Brüske, and Natascha Ueckmann, 281-295. Heidelberg: University Publishing.

Régent, Frédéric, Gilda Gonfier, and Bruno Maillard, eds. 2015. *Libres et sans fers: paroles d'esclaves français; Guadeloupe, Île Bourbon (Réunion), Martinique.* Paris: Fayard.

Rice, Alan J. 2010. *Creating Memorials, Building Identities: The Politics of Memory in the Black Atlantic.* Liverpool: Liverpool University Press.

Rodrigo y Alharilla, Martín. 2013. "De la esclavitud al cosmopolitismo. Tomás Terry Adán y su familia." *Afroamérica. Espacios e identidades,* ed. Javier Laviña, José Antonio Piqueras, and Cristina Mondéjar, 93-119. Barcelona: Icaria.

Rogers, Dominique, ed. 2015. *Voix d'esclaves. Antilles, Guyane et Louisiane françaises, XVIII-XIXe siècles.* Paris: Karthala.

Schmieder, Ulrike. 2013. "The Teaching Religious Orders and Slave Emancipation in Martinique." *Journal of Caribbean History* 47. 2: 153-183.

———. 2017. *Nach der Sklaverei – Martinique und Kuba im Vergleich.* Berlin: LIT.

———. 2018. "Sites of Memory of Atlantic Slavery in European Towns with an Excursus on the Caribbean." *Cuadernos Inter. c.a.mbio sobre Centroamérica y el Caribe* 15.1: 29-75.

"Slavery historian awarded Citizen of Honour." *Liverpool Express.* 21.07.2017. https://liverpoolexpress.co.uk/slavery-historian-awarded-citizen-of-honour/.

Smith, Laurajane et al., eds. 2011. *Representing Enslavement and Abolition in Museums. Ambiguous Engagements.* New York, London: Routledge, 2011.

Spence, David. 2011. "Making the London, Sugar & Slavery Gallery at the Museum of London Docklands." *Representing Enslavement and Abolition in Museums. Ambiguous Engagements*, ed. Laurajane Smith et al., 149-163. New York, London: Routledge.

Surwillo, Lisa. 2014. *Monsters by Trade: Slave Traffickers in Modern Spanish Literature and Culture*. Stanford: Stanford University Press.

Tibbles, Anthony. 2008. "Facing Slavery's Past: The Bicentenary of the Abolition of the British Slave Trade." *Slavery & Abolition* 29.2: 293-303.

Tin, Louis-Georges. 2013. *Esclavages et réparations. Comment faire face aux crimes de l'histoire*. Paris: Stock.

Tomich, Dale. 2004. *Through the Prism of Slavery: Labor, Capital, and World Economy*. Lanham: Rowman & Littlefield.

Tracing Centre of the DeWolf family. http://www.tracingcenter.org/.

The Trans-Atlantic Slave Trade Database (TSTD): http://www.slavevoyages.org/assessment/estimates.

Transatlantic Slavery: An Introduction. 2010. International Slavery Museum. Foreword by Rev. Jesse Jackson. Liverpool: Liverpool University Press.

Vergès, Françoise. 2015. *Liberté! Le Mémorial de l'abolition de l'esclavage*. Nantes: Éditions Château des Ducs de Bretagne.

Yacou, Alain. 1992. "Système esclavagiste: Cuba et Guadeloupe." *Commerce et Plantation dans la Caraïbe, XVIIIe et XIXe siècles*, ed. Paul Butel, 191-215. Bordeaux: Maison des pays ibériques.

———. 1994. "Los refugiados franceses de Saint-Domingue en la región occidental de la Isla." *Revista del Caribe* 23: 66-79.

Walvin, James. 2011. *Slavery and the Building of Britain*. http://www.bbc.co.uk/history/british/abolition/building_britain_gallery.shtml, last updated 17.02.2011.

Westgaph, Laurence. 2009. "Built on Slavery." *Context* 108: 29-33, httsp://ihbconline.co.uk/context/108/#29/z.

Envisioning Freedom Futures: Ernst Bloch's *not yet* and Early Eighteenth-Century Slave Societies in the Danish West Indies and Dutch Suriname

HEIKE RAPHAEL-HERNANDEZ

Abstract

The essay relates the complex and often contradictory encounters of Moravian missionaries, a Protestant group from Saxony, with enslaved Africans in the early eighteenth-century Danish West Indies and Dutch Suriname. I claim that in their mission-related contacts during this specific period, both groups would receive glimpses of secular possibilities for future societies that eventually would help bring changes to their own specific secular settings. For the enslaved Africans, it implied an insistence on freedom from the misanthropic institution of New World slavery; for the Germans, it implied a maturing of progressive ideas in regard to the still existing secular estates system. Both groups afforded each other, even if only temporarily, a vision of the *not yet*, a term German Marxist philosopher Ernst Bloch coined.

Introduction

In 1737 on the Caribbean island of St. Thomas, an enslaved woman, about to be sexually violated by one of the plantation overseers, pulled out a Bible and read to him about his sin and the eternal punishment he would receive by the laws of the white man's – i.e. *his* – religion. According to the report about this incident found in the Moravian missionary documents of 1737, her act caused him to relent.[1] In another document, a letter from 1739, seven enslaved Afri-

---

1   *Diarium* St. Thomas, 30 March 1737, Unitätsarchiv [UA] Herrnhut, Germany: R15. Ba10.

cans wrote in the name of 650 black scholars of Jesus Christ to the Danish king, Christian VI.[2] In their letter, they protested about the plantation owners' continued harassment and mistreatment of the Moravian missionaries who were working among the enslaved. Along with recounting how plantation owners burned the enslaved Africans' spelling books and how some enslaved even had their ears and feet cut off as a punishment for reading the Bible, the seven slaves specifically objected to the incarceration of two white missionaries and asked the king to show his mercy and grace by interfering with their imprisonment.[3] At the same time, they also wrote letters of encouragement to their brown brothers and sisters – these would be Native American Moravians – in Bethlehem, Pennsylvania.[4] In addition to these documents, the Moravian archival material includes *Lebensläufe* that can be regarded as small autobiographies that all Moravian members – white, black, and brown – wrote or dictated during the course of their lives, which were intended to be read at their funerals as eulogies and their last words and greetings to the congregation.

For this essay, I will focus on the encounter of enslaved Africans with early eighteenth-century Moravian missionaries, a German evangelical group from Herrnhut, Saxony. I will single out the very first Moravian missionaries who started their work among enslaved Africans in the Danish West Indies and in the Dutch colony of Suriname in the 1730s and propose the idea that both groups, the early Moravian missionaries and the enslaved Africans, inspired each other towards attitudes that contributed to a maturing political consciousness for both groups in their mission-related contacts.

The Moravian archives are not limited to texts written or dictated by enslaved and free Afro-Caribbean Moravian members themselves. In addition, there are personal letters by Moravian missionaries to their families back home in Europe and official letters

---

2   Unitätsarchiv [UA] Bethlehem, Pennsylvania: MissWI 152.7.
3   UA Bethlehem, PA: MissWI 129.2.
4   Cf., for example, UA Bethlehem, PA: MissWI 153.2.

to the Moravian church communities in Bethlehem, Pennsylvania, and Herrnhut, Upper Lusatia in today's eastern part of Germany. The missionaries diligently and meticulously reported about their daily struggles in the West Indies and Suriname; the efforts, successes, and failures of their missionary work among enslaved Africans; their frustrations with local authorities; and their first-hand impressions of slavery in the West Indies and Suriname. They also kept detailed diaries, or *diariums*.

These documents must be read critically because at no time in their history were Moravian communities themselves free of the attitudes and constraints of their immediate surroundings. For example, while Moravian missionaries themselves bought Africans for the small farms they needed for their economic survival, they never granted these members their legal freedom.[5] However, despite this fact, it was with these very early eighteenth-century Moravian missionary communities in the West Indies and Suriname that their African members, enslaved and free, experienced a disruption of racial

5   Despite their radical theology of equality, at no time in their history were Moravian communities themselves free of the secular constraints of their immediate surroundings. This fact led them to some questionable decisions throughout their history. For example, during their initial contact with slavery, Moravian leaders back in Herrnhut, Saxony struggled with the concept of slavery, but realizing that any protests would endanger their mission, they made it official church doctrine to settle for the division between physical slavery on earth and spiritual slavery in eternity. Throughout the centuries, Moravian leadership has always stressed political neutrality and encouraged members to be as politically uninvolved as possible in order to not endanger their missionary work – a dangerous and ambivalent attitude that was also observed during the Third Reich and the era of the German Democratic Republic. Concerning their attitudes toward slavery, for example, the World Council of the Moravian Church issued an official apology only as late as 1996 for several problematic attitudes they held during the era of slavery, including buying and owning slaves themselves without subsequently granting them freedom. For a detailed discussion of Moravian initial struggle with slavery, their changing attitudes over time, and changing biblical justifications, cf. Sensbach 2005; Faull 1998.

hierarchies. Because of the belief and practice of equality and respect Moravian missionaries had for all their members, African members not only learned to read and write – admittedly with the primary goal of studying holy scripture – but also held a variety of administrative and theological positions in their congregations.

I suggest that a close reading of these different documents reveals facts that the writers probably included for other purposes, yet, that allows one to detect forms of active protest and creative agency on the part of both groups: the early missionaries and enslaved people in their particular circumstances. In *Scenes of Subjection*, Saidiya Hartman asks how it is

> possible to think of 'agency' when the slave's very condition of being or social existence is defined as a state of determinate negation [...] what are the constituents of agency when one's social condition is defined by negation and personhood refigured in the fetishized and fungible terms of object of property? (1997, 52)

For Hartman,

> the particular status of the slave as object and as subject requires a careful consideration of the notion of agency [...] Certainly the constrains of agency are great in this situation, and it is difficult to imagine a way in which the interpellation of the slave as subject enables forms of agency that do not reinscribe the terms of subjugation. (54)

To respond to Hartman's concerns, I argue that agency in this particular time and space of the early Moravian missionary activities in the Danish West Indies and Suriname was possible because two things came together: Afro-Caribbeans were outside the perceived as 'objects of property' in their contact with the Moravians and they experienced a disruption of racial hierarchies. The Moravian documents offer testimony of agency born of this combination. For this essay, I carefully take Hartman's concern into my thesis and look at agency in an unusual place and time that seemingly do not allow or offer such concept. I claim that, in their mission-related contacts during this specific period, both groups would receive glimpses of secular possibilities for future societies which eventually help bring changes to their own specific secular settings. For the enslaved Africans, it implied an growing ideological insistence on an all-encompassing freedom from the misanthropic institution of New World slavery. For the Germans, it implied an awakening and maturing of progressive ideas in regard to the still existing secular estates system, which still held many Germans in either serfdom or other forms of civil bondage. Both groups afforded each other, even if this was only temporarily, a vision of the *not yet*, a term the German Marxist philosopher Ernst Bloch coined (Raphael-Hernandez 2008, 13-32). Such visions of alternative futures, even if an individual is able to only see fragments of the *not yet*, can serve as ideological empowerment. In their contact with each other during this particular time and place, the Moravian Germans and the enslaved Africans must have seen such fragments of the *not yet*, of possibilities of an alternative future. This could happen only because these first missionaries often operated with means that were not part of any official mission directives. I will demonstrate this with three aspects: the attitudes of the Moravian members toward each other inside and outside the church communities, the missionaries' approach to literacy for the enslaved, and, probably the most important empowering tool, their invalidation of white people's assumed God-given superiority in the eyes of black people. The nexus of these three aspects very likely contributed to each group's vision of a society-to-come, which, in turn, must have led more to an ideological insistence on the human right to freedom with all its different implications than has been noted so far in scholarship.

Early Moravians

The early period between the 1730s and 1760s differed from all subsequent periods of Moravian missionary presence in the Caribbean since the majority of the first Moravian missionaries to the Caribbean and Suriname came from Germany's lowest classes (Raphael-

Hernandez 2017, 458-459). Among their listed job descriptions, one finds an overwhelming number of potters, carpenters, tailors, black-smiths, brick layers, and shoemakers. The idea of sending such trades-people was a pragmatic one because the missionaries had to be fi-nancially independent from Europe and support themselves through the work they could find in the island communities where they set-tled. Craftsmen seemed to have a better chance of finding employ-ment than trained scholars of theology, who were usually members of higher classes. This fact helps to understand why the home com-munity at the headquarters in Herrnhut did not have problems with sending non-scholars to the mission field, that is, the "plain," un-educated, lower-class brothers and sisters, who were to carry out one of the most important tasks of Moravian theological essence – taking God's word to all corners of the world.

Germany, at that time, was arranged in a *Ständegesellschaft*, where individuals belonged to groups that were determined mainly by birth and were organized around a hierarchy of prestige that was arranged according to legal and social criteria (Gagliardo 1991; Sheehan 1989). While I do not imply that the living conditions of the lower classes in the German territories can be compared to the inhumane suffering of the enslaved people in the Caribbean, for my thesis it is important to note that the German system included forms of unfreedom that were based on hereditary subjection, which, among other factors, limited a person's rights to move, marry, or do certain kinds of work (Gagliardo 1991; Sheehan 1989). It is with these two rather incomparable groups, the lower-class German mis-sionaries and the enslaved Africans in the early eighteenth century, that I detect a critical nexus of spiritual matters with secular em-powerment that carried an ideological potential for both groups, al-lowing them to dream about a different future.

Such a mutual, ideological inspiration could have happened be-cause, without abandoning or disregarding official theological mat-ters, the early missionaries in the West Indies and Suriname unoffi-cially seemed to have taken St. Paul's spiritual statement of "There is neither Jew nor Gentile, neither slave nor free, nor is there male

and female, for you are all one in Christ Jesus" from Galatians 3:28
to the secular realm. As part of their group's theology, Moravians
practiced a Christian ideal that was based on the New Testament, but
for their time, it was unusual and rather radical. Inside their church
community, all Moravians, regardless of class, gender, or race, were
of equal standing and treated each other with the same respect. Outside their church community, however, Moravians in the mission
field were supposed to observe the social arrangements in regard to
the class and racial divisions of plantation societies. Yet, as I will
show, quite a few of these early missionaries were siding with black
people against white people in matters that were not related to theological aspects or church work. As a consequence of this transfer of
spiritual equality to the secular realm, both groups afforded each
other, even if this was only temporarily, a vision of the *not yet*.

Bloch's *not yet*

According to Bloch's theory, visions of possible alternative futures,
of societies-to-come, will serve as ideological empowerment for the
individual, even if an individual is able to see only fragments of the
not yet (Raphael-Hernandez 2008, 13-32). Since Bloch does not
have the desires of individuals and their limited wish fulfillment in
mind, rather the liberation of the whole human race, he adds *collective existence* to this political vision. Glimpses of the *not yet* will,
for example, cause a hungry person to not only search for food for
themselves, but also to change the situation that caused the hunger
in the first place for the entire community, a motivation Bloch refers
to as *revolutionary interest*. Revolutionary interest coupled with the
individual's glimpses of the *not yet* serve as *pre-appearance*. This
differs from illusion since an illusion is removed from reality whereas the foundation for Bloch's *pre-appearance* is an individual person's reality; the person will be able to begin to act in his or her reality. As humans, in difference to the divine, we are not able to envision or anticipate the future in its fullest, only in fragments or
glimpses. But even these fragments of the *not yet* are powerful

enough to let someone experience an ideologically empowered hope and begin to change their respective present circumstances. All such activities or events intended to affect change contained a *spiritual surplus*. Tom Moylan explains Bloch's idea of the *surplus*: "In each victory of the human project there remains a specific type of hope which is not that of the present and which carries that victorious moment beyond itself, anticipating the next one" (Moylan 1982, 160). This *spiritual surplus*, also called *utopian surplus*, allows a specific event or activity to transcend its particular period and connect with the ultimate universal human ability to strive toward changes. Bloch sees the *utopian surplus* in every field of human creativity (25). The *utopian surplus* is closely connected to another concept, the *novum*. The *novum* stands for the "new" aspect in every action and contains the substance that is worth saving for the future. In this regard, Bloch differentiates between *true* and *untrue future*. *Untrue future* includes all acts that will happen in the future as a mere repetition of acts that have already happened before. If, for example, a person will get up, have breakfast, and go to work tomorrow, they might consider today these events as the future, but they imply *untrue future* because they do not provide any novelty. Only acts that have not happened before can be part of *true future*. The *utopian surplus* is connected with *true future* because it embodies the visions of completely new circumstances that have not existed before in history. For the Marxist Bloch, of course, the goal of "man en route" is the transformation of the world into a place without any discrimination or oppression, where human self-realization can reach its fullest potential and "man is walking upright" (Plaice 1986, xxxiii). Contrary to Marx, Bloch believes that the individual is the prime mover of history. Bloch emphasizes vehemently the importance of human agency rooted in individual consciousness. According to Bloch, every person is equipped with a subconscious ability to anticipate the future. He calls this ability to envision the future, or to get a glimpse of the *not-yet-become*, the *anticipatory illumination* or the *anticipatory consciousness*. The anticipatory ability is closely connected to hope, in this case, "hope is not taken only as emotion, as the opposite of fear … but more essentially as a directing act of a cognitive kind" (Bloch 1986, 12). Because it connects hope with reason, the *anticipatory consciousness* connects the expectant emotions to their utopian function. Bloch emphasizes repeatedly that he does not talk about an egocentric hope that has in mind only private gains and advantages. For his theory, he deals with the hope that wants to change the world. Bloch's ultimate goal is the human society in which subject and object no longer face each other as strangers. Virginio Marzocchi emphasizes that although Bloch usually uses the terms "individual," "self-realization," and "subject," he does not have the limited individual's own small desires in mind (1985, 198). Bloch's individual realizes that their own future is inseparably connected to the fate of society at large.

Inside and Outside: The Moravian Church Community and *not yet*

To locate such fragments of the *not yet* for the two chosen groups in this essay, one needs to look at two important arenas: their interactions inside and outside the church community. Inside the church, all members, regardless of their class, gender, race, or social status, were equal. Moravians based their idea on St. Paul's above-mentioned premise that there would be "neither slave nor free" because all would be "one in Christ." This was not just a secret favorite verse of some missionaries, but one of the main doctrines of Moravian theology. Throughout their own history, Moravians have tried to practice this divine call to equality. It meant that Afro-Moravians belonged as equals to the larger community of all "mankind" via the smaller community of the Moravian church. And indeed, African members, free and enslaved, held a variety of administrative and theological positions in their congregations; enslaved Africans became deacons, elders, and helpers in mixed-race communities. The practiced cross-racial and cross-class equality inside their church community can also be seen in the way they addressed each other. Moravians, white as well as black members, expressed their respect for each other by addressing each other with the terms "Brother" and "Sister." They write about "Br. Petrus," "Br. Abraham," "Br. Johannes," and "Br. Cornelius." In the few letters available in the archives that were written by black members, the writers signed with these brotherly and sisterly titles of love, respect, and belonging. They, as "Br. Cornelius" does, send their greetings to "Br. Nathaniel" and "Br. Johan."[6] Afro-Moravian "Isaac and his Rebecca, Nathanael, Jacob, Paulina, Anna Louisa" send "their affectionate greetings" to all brothers and sisters in the church community.[7]

With these examples, one recognizes the first opportunities of Bloch's *not yet* to help create and nurture a secular political imagination. The glimpses of the *not yet* inside the church community provided the ideological tool for activating resistance for the outside secular everyday imagination. I will show this further with two aspects.

Literacy as Weapon

One example of an aspect that began with spiritual intentions but turned into secular empowerment can be seen in the joint attitude of enslaved Africans and missionaries toward literacy and its application in rather subversive agendas. The missionaries, who often had only rudimentary levels of literacy themselves,[8] taught the enslaved to read and write – admittedly with the primary goal of studying holy

6   Cf. material in folders for MissWI 152, MissWI 153, MAB, and MissSur 14, MAB; the two examples are MissWI 153.1, MAB, and MissWI 153.2, MAB.

7   The German original reads: "bitten gar sehr herzlich die Gemeine zu grüßen" (MissWI 160.4, MAB).

8   The following excerpt from Dober's *diarium* can serve as example for the claim of rudimentary literacy; the text does not follow any conventional requirements for German spelling rules. The German original reads: "Sankt Thomas den 16. Aprill 1733 Gieng bruder Nitschman an bort. Den 17. früh gieng das Schief unter Seegel. Zu abent besucht ich die Anna und Abraham" (UA, R.15.B.a.2.b.2, Unitäts-Archiv, Herrnhut, Germany).

scripture – because according to Pietist notions, one has to be able to read the Bible in order to engage with God's word regularly in small weekly discussion groups. However, with their idea of enabling the enslaved to read and write, the missionaries came into conflict with the official Danish 'slave code' for the islands that forbade literacy for enslaved people. In addition, it is important to note that while the missionaries' acts might not have violated Moravian theology, they definitely acted against the secular rules their leader Count von Zinzendorf set up for the mission field. This becomes obvious by his reaction to their idea: in a letter of 1736 to another missionary group, the Moravian missionaries to the Samoyed in Siberia, Zinzendorf wrote, "Under no circumstances involve yourself in external affairs other than work. The Brethren on St. Thomas are teaching the Moors to write, we disapprove of this completely. One can arouse the anger of the authorities with such a small thing" (Uttendörfer 1913, 9).

   In a later nineteenth-century text, Frederick Douglass, a former American enslaved person, reports about the enslaved Africans' own awareness of the empowerment that reading could provide for them. Douglass recalls that he gave pieces of bread to hungry white children so that they would teach him how to read, which leads him to exclaim, "The more I read, the more I was led to abhor and detest my enslavers" (Douglass 1845, 40). In the Moravian documents, we learn about much earlier instances of enslaved Africans' strong desires to become literate (cf. Hall 1992). One repeatedly finds in the letters and diaries of the missionaries that many of them seem only to be coming to the Christian meetings in order to learn to read and write (Oldendorp 2002, 166). They will not sit still and listen when they learn about the blood that Christ sacrificed for them, it is reported, but instead seem to want to hurry the missionaries up to get to the part where they teach them how to spell. The missionaries' reaction shows that most of them were rather torn between their support of the enslaved Africans' desire and their own wish to bring first and foremost the Christian message to them. In their texts, the missionaries frequently express their concern that many of the enslaved seem to be interested in literacy only for secular gains. One measure introduced to prevent this problem was moving the spelling instructions to the latter part of the evening after Bible instructions, hoping that this would deter all but the very sincere from attending. At a certain point, the missionaries even tried limiting these spelling lessons to those who were close to being converted (Oldendorp 2002, 166, 177, 185, 187, 210). Yet, all this was to no avail; the enslaved indeed had discovered the secular power of literacy. Still, even if several missionaries worried that they were taken advantage of by the enslaved, and even if many enslaved and maroons saw that they were being lured into Christianity via literacy, both groups, in obvious cooperation, used literacy for secular empowerment in their respective circumstances. This claim can be illustrated with the example of the enslaved Africans' use of passes during slave revolts. While official Moravian church policies urged their members not to get involved in protests or even in revolts, the written discourse about these events allows one to speculate about how a creative protest could have taken place. In the documents, one reads repeatedly about slave uprisings or about rumors of slave revolts and about panicked planters who forbade enslaved from leaving their plantations. Together with white Moravians, the enslaved Moravian members often asked for "exception passes" so that they would be able to attend church meetings. Especially evening meetings that would cause slaves to return after dark were regarded as suspicious activities by plantation owners. Being fully aware of the planters' fears, Moravians wrote passes for hundreds of them, and one can only speculate that they were not used exclusively for attending evening church gatherings in town. In one planter's diary, it is report about a particular incident when the enslaved were not allowed to leave their plantations because of the rumor of an imminent slave revolt. Nevertheless, as the planter records, he saw at least 200 black people on their way to Posaunenberg, the Moravian church in St. Thomas (Hall 1992, 112). In another report for the year 1750, it is reported about several slave revolts in St. Thomas and a subsequent ban on leaving plantations after dark. Concerned that their members would not be able to participate in church meetings, the missionaries were able to get an exception to this order for all enslaved who would show passes with Moravian signatures. One of their Afro-Moravian members, Mingo, was then tasked to write and also sign these passes. Furthermore, the report notes that during subsequent times of revolts and rumors of rebellions, the white missionaries simply left it to Mingo to write and sign these passes without checking on him (Oldendorp 2002, 856).[9]

Eternal Slavery and the Invalidation of White Superiority

One of the best examples that must have contributed tremendously to a vision of the *not yet* can be observed with the missionaries' attitude toward sinning. Their raging about spiritual matters in regard to sinning must have caused something that was of essential importance to a growing secular political awareness among enslaved people; white Moravians took away white people's assumed God-given superiority, thus taking away white people's unimpeachable invulnerability in the eyes of black people.

For the missionaries, St. Paul's words, "neither slave nor free [...] you are all one in Christ Jesus," implied that to sin or not to sin was a concern that applied equally to blacks as well as whites. One can see this with the example of how the missionaries handled dancing, drumming, and promiscuous behaviour. The missionaries were often very angry with the enslaved because they considered these activities forms of sin that separated a person from God. In their letters and diaries, the missionaries constantly lament that even slaves who have been baptized and are now Afro-Moravian members go

---

9 Hilary Beckles points out an additional use of slave passes. According to his research, it was indeed common for slaves to write their own passes, thus offering an opportunity for escape to runaway slaves who could use these counterfeit passes to travel to neighboring islands. Once there, they could reinvent themselves as freedmen in such port towns as Charlotte Amalie in St. Thomas, which had a large community of free black people; cf. Beckles 2000, 1011.

back to their old ways and enjoy dancing and drumming on Satur-
day nights. According to the missionaries, slave dances were part of
African heathen cultures. In their *diaria*, one reads about many incidents in which the missionaries punished members by placing them
on "probation," thus excluding them from communion and even ex-
pelling those who did not show remorse for their action after a certain period of time. However, it is of crucial importance that they
also showed the same zeal when telling black people about white
people's behavior and sin. They often raged viciously against white
planters' sinful behavior and repeatedly told enslaved black people
that these free white people would be damned to eternal slavery in
hell for their adultery and sexual exploitation of black women. Already the very first two missionaries, Leonard Dober and David
Nitschmann, told the enslaved they came into contact with that white
plantation owners who call themselves Christian, but leave their
wives behind in Europe and force enslaved women into sexual relationships with them, would not belong to Christ but to the devil.[10]
One repeatedly finds texts that report how enslaved women com-
plained to the missionaries about their sexual exploitation by plantation owners and white workers and the missionaries clearly took a
stance against white people in these cases, openly declaring that
these white men will be judged for their sins, as God does not differentiate between 'slave or free' in making his judgment. They
even encouraged enslaved women to use this thought as a spiritual
weapon against their tormentors. Such an example is in a *diarium*
entry for St. Thomas in 1737, describing how an enslaved woman,
about to be sexually violated by one of the plantation overseers,
pulled out a Bible and read to him about his sin and the eternal punishment he would receive by the laws of the white man's – i.e. *his* –
religion. According to the report, her act caused him to relent.[11]

---

10 Cf., for example, Leonard Dober and David Nitschmann, *Diarium*, St.
    Thomas, Januarius 1733: "wir sagten ihm aber daß die nicht Christo
    sondern dem Teuffel angehörten." Cf. Kröger 2006, 49, 53, 55, 56, 59.

11 *Diarium*, St. Thomas, 30 March 1737 (UA R15. Ba10, Unitäts-Archiv
    Herrnhut, Germany).

Such rhetorical encouragements as these might not have been in conflict with the Moravians' official policy of non-involvement in any secular politics, yet, they must have caused something else that was of essential importance to slave resistance and rebellion; they took away white people's spiritual and mental superiority in the eyes of black people. This fact cannot be emphasized enough because, after all, both groups were still part of a historical period in which religious beliefs were fundamental and one's assumed individual judgment by God could still cause existential fears.

Conclusion

Beginning in the 1770s, Moravian missionaries slowly began to give up their initially radical attitudes and moved instead toward friendly cooperation with the planter class. Instead of breaking bread with the enslaved in their huts or inviting them into their homes to share their own food with them, as the first missionaries practiced, they now dined at the master's table. In later missionary reports from Suriname, one can often read about incidents when missionaries acted as the henchmen of plantation directors by telling slaves to obey their masters' orders to work on Sundays, the only day that was work-free for enslaved people (Lamur 2000). In addition, quite a few of the later missionaries also discovered a secular taste for slavery's profits, thus sacrificing religious zeal for monetary gain and greed. It is a well-known fact that Moravian missionaries of later decades were siding more with plantation owners than with the enslaved people; quite a few became ardent slave holders themselves. During the later decades until emancipation, the Moravian narrative of earlier ideals of dignity, respect, and equality abandoned acquires a tragic overtone (Sensbach 1998; Lamur 2000; Hüsgen 2016). For the early group, however, one can safely assume that when the early missionaries started their assignments, they had not developed secular oppositional stances toward slavery because their leader, Count von Zinzendorf, would not have endorsed their call to the mission field. The missionaries' secular consciousness grew while working together with the enslaved; a maturing political consciousness happened therefore to both groups in mutual encouragement. Because of their Pietist theology and radical forms of practiced Christianity in secular settings, wittingly as well as unwittingly, the early Moravians and the enslaved inspired each other, thus contributing to a political consciousness and offering visions of the *not yet* that would eventually lead to their insistence of an all-encompassing and unconditional human right to freedom in their respective societies.

Archives

Moravian Archives, Bethlehem, PA, U.S.A. (MAB), MissWI (Missions in the West Indies collection).
Moravian Archives, Bethlehem, PA, U.S.A. (MAB), MissSur (Missions in Suriname collection)
Unitäts-Archiv, Herrnhut, Germany (UA).

Works Cited

Beckles, Hilary McDonald. 2000. "Persistent Rebels: Women and Anti-Slavery Activity." *Caribbean Slavery in the Atlantic World*, ed. Verene Shepherd and Hilary McDonald Beckles, 1001-1016. Kingston: Ian Randle Publishers.
Bloch, Ernst. 1986. *The Principle of Hope*. Trans. Neville Plaice, Stephen Plaice, and Paul Knight. Oxford: Basil Blackwell.
Douglass, Frederick. 1845. *Narrative of the Life of Frederick Douglass, an American Slave. Written by Himself.* Boston: Anti-Slavery Office.
Faull, Katherine M. 1998. "Self-Encounters: Two Eighteenth-Century African Memoirs from Moravian Bethlehem." *Crosscurrents: African Americans, Africa, and Germany in the Modern World*, ed. David McBride, Leroy Hopkins, and C. Aisha Blackshire-Belay, 29-52. New York: Camden House.

Gagliardo, John. 1991. *Germany under the Old Regime, 1600-1790.* London: Longman.

Hall, Neville A.T. 1992. *Slave Society in the Danish West Indies.* Baltimore: The Johns Hopkins University Press.

Hartman, Saidiya. 1997. *Scenes of Subjection: Terror, Slavery, and Self-Making in Nineteenth-Century America.* New York: Oxford University Press.

Hüsgen, Jan. 2016. *Mission und Sklaverei: Die Herrnhuter Brüdergemeine und die Sklavenemanzipation in Britisch- und Dänisch-Westindien.* Stuttgart: Franz Steiner Verlag.

Kröger, Rüdiger, ed. 2006. *Johann Leonard Dober und der Beginn der Herrnhuter Mission.* Herrnhut: Comenius-Buchhandlung.

Lamur, Humphrey. 2000. "Slave Religion on the Vossenburg Plantation (Suriname) and Missionaries' Reactions." *Caribbean Slavery in the Atlantic World,* ed. Verene Shepherd and Hilary McDonald Beckles, 714-721. Kingston: Ian Randle Publishers.

Marzocchi, Virginio. 1985. "Utopie als 'Novum' und 'letzte Wiederholung' bei Ernst Bloch." *Ernst Bloch. Text und Kritik,* ed. Heinz Ludwig Arnold, 194-207. München: edition text + kritik.

Moylan, Tom. 1982. "The Locus of Hope: Utopia versus Ideology." *Science-Fiction Studies* 9: 159-166.

Oldendorp, Christian Georg Andreas. 2002. *Historie der caribischen Inseln Sanct Thomas, Sanct Crux und Sanct Jan, insbesondere der dasigen Neger und der Mission der Evangelischen Brüder unter denselben. Zweiter Teil: Die Missionsgeschichte,* ed. Hartmut Beck, Gudrun Meier, Stephan Palmié, Aart H. van Soest, Peter Stein, and Horst Ulbricht. Berlin: Verlag für Wissenschaft und Bildung.

———. 1777. *Geschichte der Mission der evangelischen Brüder auf den caribischen Inseln S. Thomas, S. Croix und S. Jan,* ed. Johann Jakob Bossard. Barby: Friedrich Christoph Laux.

Plaice, Neville, Stephen Plaice, and Paul Knight. 1986. "Translators' Introduction." *The Principle of Hope* by Ernst Bloch, Xix-xxxiii. Oxford: Basil Blackwell.

Raphael-Hernandez, Heike. 2017. "The Right to Freedom: Eighteenth-Century Slave Resistance and Early Moravian Missions in the Danish West Indies and Dutch Suriname." *Atlantic Studies Journal* 14.4 (Special Issue "German Entanglements in Transatlantic Slavery", ed. Heike Raphael-Hernandez and Pia Wiegmink): 457-475.

———. 2008. *The Utopian Aesthetics of Three African American Women (Toni Morrison, Gloria Naylor, Julie Dash): The Principle of Hope.* Lewiston, NY: The Edwin Mellen Press.

Sensbach, Jon. 1998. *A Separate Canaan: The Making of an Afro-Moravian World in North Carolina, 1763-1840.* Chapel Hill: University of North Carolina Press.

———. 2005. *Rebecca's Revival: Creating Black Christianity in the Atlantic World.* Cambridge: Harvard University Press.

Sheehan, James J. 1989. *German History 1770-1866.* Oxford: Clarendon Press.

Uttendörfer, Otto. 1913. *Die wichtigsten Missionsinstruktionen Zinzendorfs.* Herrnhut: Verlag der Missionsbuchhandlung.

The Link of a Former British Prime Minister's Ancestor to Caribbean Slavery Economy in the Current Call for Reparations in Jamaica

CLAUDIA RAUHUT

Abstract

This paper examines current reactions of Jamaican activists for slavery reparations in relation to research that uncovered the profits that the British elite, among them the ancestor of the former British Prime Minister David Cameron, gained by the compensation paid to British slave-owners at the end of slavery. It reflects on a public media scandal in relation to a bank loan that once financed these large payments and that was paid off only in 2015. Based on empirical research in Kingston, the paper analyzes how the activists organized under the National Council for Reparations in Jamaica used this information to strengthen their political agenda on behalf of slavery reparations and how in particular they countered the British position of denial of recognition of the legacies of slavery. They are part of the political campaign led by the CARICOM Reparations Commission, a transregional organization composed by civil society activists from Anglophone Caribbean States. Since 2013, this commission calls upon European governments, successor states of the colonial powers that invested in and profited from the slave trade and slavery, to apologize and engage in a process of reparations.

Jamaican and Anglophone Caribbean Activism in Favor of Slavery Reparations

Within my current research, I came across archival information that uncovered not only the tremendous profits that British slave owners gained through their involvement in the Caribbean slavery economy, as well as the large compensation for "loss of property" they received when slavery was abolished in 1833. One of the slave owners was the ancestor of the former British Prime Minister David Cameron – a piece of information that is not particularly astonishing. Remarkable, however, is the fact that when Cameron visited Jamaica in 2015, he rejected any talks about the slavery past and reparations – a position that was publicly scandalized not only by the reparation activists. Another public outrage came from a tweet the British Treasury posted in February 2018 stating that British citizens "helped to end the slave trade by their taxes" by paying off a loan until the year 2015 – without making any reference to the fact that this loan was used to compensate the slave-owners instead of the enslaved. This tweet involuntarily provided a relevant detail that shed new light on the ongoing legacies of the compensation process and provided fresh momentum for the reparations case in Jamaica.

In this paper, I analyze how Jamaican activists countered both public statements by transforming it into a broader political mobilization on behalf of reparations. I emphasize the public reactions and media discourses in relation to Cameron's statement of denial and new research on the compensation process and related bank loan. This essay is part of my broader research on transregional perspectives on Caribbean activism for slavery reparations[1] where I have conducted ethnographic interviews with members of the National Council on Reparations (NCR) in Jamaica in 2014 and 2017. This council in Jamaica – a country that is a forerunner for reparations struggle in the Caribbean and globally – was founded with the support of the Jamaican government in 2009. It is composed by scholars of the University of the West Indies, by lawyers, human rights activists, journalists and Rastafarians.[2] They are part of the political campaign led by the CARICOM Reparations Commission, a trans-

---

1   At Freie Universität Berlin, funded by the Fritz Thyssen Foundation.

2   For the history of the Jamaican reparations movement including the pivotal role of Rastafarians, cf. Rauhut 2018b. An overview of the global history of reparations activism is provided by Araujo 2017; Beckles 2013; *Journal of African American History* 2018.

regional organization basically composed by civil society activists from Anglophone Caribbean States which were former British colonies. Since 2013, this commission calls upon European governments, mostly Great Britain for the moment, but also France, Spain, Portugal, the Netherlands, and Denmark, as successor states of the colonial powers that invested in and profited from the slave trade and slavery to apologize and engage in a process of reparations, sought here as infrastructural investments within Caribbean societies.[3] Exemplified by the case of Jamaica, I have analyzed the arguments and narratives of the members of the NCR who reconstruct the legacies of slavery and colonialism in order to advocate for present responsibilities to repair the injustices of the past. I have identified the various dimensions of their agenda: campaigns within public education for a rewriting of the slavery past in relation to its current legacies, countering the conventional modernist development discourse, and mobilizing transnational networks for reparations in order to strengthen their claims (Rauhut 2018a, 2018b, 2018c). As a crucial aspect, I have analyzed their narratives of injustices that redress the compensation paid to the slave-owners by the British parliament in the 1830s as current ground for their claims (Rauhut forthcoming). This contribution focuses particularly on their public answers to Cameron's position of denial and starts by providing an overview of respective research on the compensation process and related bank loan.

The Impact of Researching the Compensation of British Slave Owners in the 1830s

When slavery was finally abolished in the British colonies in the Caribbean by the 'Slavery Abolition Act' in 1833, the British plantation and slave owners only agreed after claiming compensation for the loss of property, as they considered their slaves as property or

---

3   CARICOM Reparations Commission 2014: "10-Point Reparation Plan," http://caricomreparations.org/caricom/caricoms-10-point-reparation--plan/.

movable chattels they had paid for. The British parliament, itself composed of members of a social elite who had links to the slavery economy, agreed and paid £20 million to the planters (Draper 2010). In contrast, the enslaved persons entered freedom without any compensation for the injuries suffered, without land, without property, and without any capital to build a new life. They were not even truly free as the British introduced the system of apprenticeship that forced the now formally free people for another period of 4 years (originally designed for 12 years) to remain working in the plantations, very often for the same masters, without being paid (Hall, D. G. 1953; Wilmot 1984). Historians from the Caribbean have conducted research about the compensation process in the 1980s, including my interview partner Verene Shepherd, who has led the Jamaican National Council for Reparations since 2012 (Higman 1976; Shepherd 1988; Butler 1995). However, for a broader public audience beyond academia, particularly in Europe, this information became only known when the online database *Legacies of British Slave-ownership* was launched by the British historians Catherine Hall, Nicholas Draper, and their research team from University College London in 2013, followed by joint publications.[4] The database relies foremost on Draper's book *The Price of Emancipation: Slave-ownership, Compensation and British Society at the End of Slavery* (2010). Based on immense archival research, Draper has analyzed the compensation records administered by the 'Slave Compensation Commission' between the years 1834 and 1845 and provides lists of individuals and corporations who benefitted from slavery, including "large scale and small scale slave-owners," merchants, bankers, rentiers, clergy, nobles, and Members of Parliament. According to this material, half of the total £20 million were paid to British absentee owners – they owned enslaved people and plantations in the Caribbean but never lived there. By focusing on

---

4   Centre for the Study of the Legacies of British Slave-ownership. https://www.ucl.ac.uk/lbs/. Cf. Hall, Catherine et al. 2014; Hall, Catherine, Draper, and McClelland 2014.

these absentee owners, how much compensation money they received, and what they did with this money, Draper shows that most of the profit was reinvested in Great Britain and stimulated a burst of economic growth in the mid-nineteenth century (Draper 2010, 8). The central contribution of the book is that it traces back the consequences of the compensation in terms of an inter-generational transfer of capital in cash, investment, and social status. It further highlights the fact that slave ownership was not marginal, but central to British society in the 1830s, where a large majority of the British elite had financial or familiar ties to slavery.

The scholars of the *Legacies of British Slave-Ownership* were already aware that their project "inevitably bears on the international discussion of restitution or reparations for slavery" (Draper 2010, 12) and that, even if as historians they avoid political positions, they "understand that there are potential implications of our work for the debates around these issues" (Hall, Catherine et al. 2014). The implications seem evident: the results clearly identify the individuals who received different, in some cases enormous, amounts of money and demonstrate the consecutive investments they undertook. This finally allows us to establish links between those persons and influential economic, political, financial, cultural, and religious institutions still in place today. Such evidence obviously raises questions of accountability and provides more specific grounds for the reparations argument. Draper was concerned "to locate the accountability for slavery more precisely," focusing on specific individuals, firms, banks, credit systems, and specific links to the British state, instead of assuming a sort of "systemic collective responsibility of white Britain" (Draper 2010, 14). Finally, the historians understand their emphasis on individual slave ownership as "complementary to studies of the systemic effects of slavery on the economy and of the British state," acknowledging that the empirical evidence "will be of use to many other researchers – including descendants of the enslaved who are concerned to seek forms of reparation."[5] Caribbean

---

5   https://www.ucl.ac.uk/lbs/project/context/.

activists definitely make use of the database and other related research to underline their arguments, for instance Sir Hilary Beckles,
chair of the CRC, Vice Chancellor of the UWI, and the most distinguished spokesperson for the case. He has closely collaborated with
the Jamaican activists for years. In his book *Britain's Black Debt.
Reparations for Caribbean Slavery and Native Genocide* (2013),
which has become a sort of guidebook for Caribbean and global
reparations advocates, he draws intensely on Draper's research and
reinforces the thesis of intrinsic interrelation between the British industrialization, the slave trade, Caribbean slavery, *and* compensation (Beckles 2013). Beckles and Shepherd were invited to speak at
UCL or at the Centre for the Study of International Slavery at the
University of Liverpool while Catherine Hall and her team gave
seminars at the University of the West Indies. Hall and Draper ac-
knowledge Shepherd "for her commitment to connecting the project
with initiatives in the Caribbean" (Hall, Catherine et al. 2014) –
which are in this case clearly those concerned with reparations.

David Cameron's Family Links to Caribbean Slavery and British Politics of Non-Recognition

Among those who benefited were also the ancestors of prominent
personalities such as authors Graham Greene, George Orwell, and
finally David Cameron, Great Britain's Prime Minister from 2010 to
2016. General Sir James Duff, his cousin six times removed, received compensation for the 202 enslaved people he owned at a
sugar plantation in Jamaica. This information was immediately circulated and turned into a scandal by reparations activists as well as
by media in the Caribbean and Great Britain.[6] What fanned the in-
dignation was not only the extremely large amount of money that
the British parliament transferred to slave owners (according to the
research findings, £20 million represented 40% of the total national

---

6   Randall, February 26, 2013. Cf. http://archive.indianexpress.com/news/
     david-camerons-ancestors-had-owned-slaves-report/1081072/.

budget in 1834) but also the fact that one of them was the ancestor of Prime Minister Cameron himself. This information clearly uncovered the links of Cameron's ancestors in the Caribbean, particularly the Jamaican slavery economy. With regard to the campaigns for reparations, this was a turning point in terms of mobilization, in particular when Cameron visited the island in September 2015. For my interview partners, it was exactly the right moment to spread again the relevant information through public activities, as well as through national and international media. On the eve of his visit, the NCR organized a public lecture on September 29 on Reparations in Liberty Hall in Kingston where, according to speaker Rupert Lewis, over 400 people attended, some of them wearing T-Shirts "Mr. Cameron say sorry."[7]

Various members of the NCR, among them the lawyer Bert Samuels, appealed to Cameron as an individual and as head of a former enslaving state: "he needs to atone, to apologize personally and on behalf of his country" (Dunkley, September 30, 2015). Beckles also addressed him as "a grandson of the Jamaican soil who has been privileged and enriched by your forebears' sins of the enslavement of our ancestors" in an open letter on September 26, 2015 (fully published in both Jamaican dailies). He pointed out Britain's share in the "monumental mess of Empire" left in the Caribbean and connects this share of the past to a political responsibility to share the present duties (*The Gleaner*, September 27, 2015; *Jamaica Observer*, September 28, 2015). A short time before, the Jamaican parliament had approved a two-party motion brought in by Minister Mike Henry who is a strong advocate for reparations among Jamaican politicians. Lawyer Phipps explained to me that this parliamentary motion affirms that the government of Jamaica not only supports, but is going to seek reparations from Great Britain – yet only the appropriate legal and political form is currently discussed.[8] Based on this motion and the public activities of the NCR, Simpson

---

7   Interview with Rupert Lewis, March 2, 2017.
8   Interview with Frank Phipps, March 9, 2017.

Miller has finally raised the issue of reparations when meeting
Cameron (*The Gleaner*, September 29, 2015). Rupert Lewis wel-
comed this statement and for a short moment it brought hope for a
potential shift of political relationship between the U.K. and Jamaica concerning the matter of redress: "It was the first time in our history that our political leaders stood up and said to the British Government, 'We don't agree with your denial of the justice of the
claim for reparations!'"[9] According to Lewis, whereas 2015 was "a
good year for the reparations case," all hope was broken down by
the election of Trump and the Brexit referendum in the year 2016.
The government of Theresa May seemed even more hostile and the
researchers of the NCR, as Lewis told me, could not find a personal
link between May's ancestors and Caribbean slavery – a fact that he
considers as less favorable in terms of political mobilization. Cameron, whose links to slavery had been fully proved, deliberately
failed to answer the Jamaican reparations call when he spoke in the
Jamaican parliament on September 30, 2015:

> I acknowledge that these wounds run very deep indeed. But I do
> hope that, as friends who have gone through so much together since
> those darkest of times, we can move on from this painful legacy and
> continue to build for the future.[10]

Britain's constant rejection of reparations echoes the position of European governments, which have until now systematically ignored
or rejected the various calls for reparations of their former colonies.
Jamaican activists already point to a missed opportunity in the year
2007, when the former Prime Minister Tony Blair and the Queen
avoided any apology to the people of the Caribbean during the commemoration activities and celebrations of the bicentenary of abolition of the slave trade. The Jamaica National Bicentenary Committee, a sort of precursor to the NCR, has further criticized the UK's

---

9   Interview with Rupert Lewis, March 2, 2017.
10   Government of the United Kingdom, Prime Minister's Office, Septem-
     ber 30, 2015.

strong focus on abolition as a selective way of remembering that risks erasing from the public memory the preceding 300 years of enrichment by means of a brutal system of exploitation of Africans (Shepherd et al. 2012).

Jamaican Answers to the British Proposal of "Let's Move on"

Cameron's statement in 2015 was definitely perceived as an affront that went far beyond the context of the NCR and resulted in many reactions of disagreement in international media.[11] My Jamaican interview partners were outraged and found this position extremely insulting. During my research in March 2017, one and a half years after Cameron's visit to Jamaica, they expressed their strong disapproval:

> Cameron is by blood related to a slave-owner ... and he is coming out that we should walk away and forget the past? That was an insult to us! So we felt ... he had the scorn and the disrespect for people who were enslaved![12]

> Oh well, we have come a long way as friends! And his forebears benefitted from slavery, because they were directly involved! So they [the British government] are actually tying themselves up ... I mean, those arguments are not sustainable![13]

They not only protested against Cameron's refusal to apologize and hold any reparations talk, they felt in particular affronted by the terminology of "friends" and "forget the past" he used as someone who had directly benefitted from slavery and did nothing to distance himself from it. They consequently dismantle British politics and

---

11   Beyond the Jamaican dailies also *The Guardian*, *New York Times* and BBC have largely reported about this (Bilefsky, September 30, 2015; Dunkley, September 30, 2015).

12   Interview with Bert Samuels, March 7, 2017.

13   Interview with Clinton Hutton, March 13, 2017.

the ideology of "move on" as cynical and false: "Mr. Cameron himself had slaves here. And he had the avarice to come and say, 'move
on'? This was an affront to us! But he has put the spark for a much
stronger backing for reparations within the population!"[14]

I do not know if Frank Phipps unconsciously or intentionally
stated that "Cameron himself had slaves." One might interpret this
expression as a rhetorical style that underlines a crucial argument
for reparations: It doesn't matter if it was Cameron himself or his
ancestor who received the money. What remains is the long-term
link, the fact that generations have benefitted in continuity through
slavery and compensation. Moreover, even if Cameron had not
profited directly as an individual, as Prime Minister of the successor
state of the principal European enslaving power, he could have been
engaged in a dialogue by the political-legal principle of transgene-
rational responsibility of states. My interlocutors classified Cameron's statement as a scandal but at the same time as an "incident"
that has "lightened up the road for the reparations movement."[15]
They further observed that the outreach activities of the NCR and
the intense media documentation about Cameron's involvement in
Caribbean slavery have widened the public knowledge about the
compensation payments in the 1830s, followed by diverse resent-
ments and reactions of protest.

How a Bank Loan for Ending Slavery Haunts the Present

The public scandal in reaction to Cameron's position of denial was
again highlighted in international media when historians uncovered
a relevant detail of the compensation process. It started with the article "When will Britain face up its crimes against humanity?", published in *The Guardian* on March 29, 2018, which critically engages
with a tweet the Treasury of Her Majesty posted on February 9,
2018:

---

14 Interview with Frank Phipps, March 9, 2017.
15 Interview with Rupert Lewis, March 2, 2017.

> Here's today's surprising #FridayFact. Millions of you have helped
> end the slave trade through your taxes. Did you know? In 1833,
> Britain used £20 million, 40% of its national budget, to buy free-
> dom for all slaves in the Empire. The amount of money borrowed
> for the Slavery Abolition Act was so large that it wasn't paid off un-
> til 2015. Which means that living British citizens helped pay to end
> the slave trade. (Manjapra, March 29, 2018)

Reactions of protest immediately followed and the Treasury deleted
the tweet after 24 hours. But the information was already in the air
and was quickly scandalized in British and Caribbean media. In his
essay, Kris Manjapra, Professor of History at Tufts University, deconstructs the falsity and cynical nature of the tweet. First, it was
not the slave trade (which the British had prohibited in 1807), but
slavery that was abolished in 1833. Furthermore, no freedom was
brought to the enslaved, in fact they faced similar conditions to
slavery even after its formal end. The implementation of a harsh
system of forced labor through apprenticeship increased the level of
exploitation, punishment, and torture. Therefore, instead of afford-
ing a new life without bonds to the now freed people, "the process
of emancipation marked a new phase of British atrocities and the
terrorization of blacks" (Manjapra, March 29, 2018). We therefore
must carefully counter the impression the tweet creates. First of all,
what is not mentioned or disparately decontextualized is that "to
buy freedom for all slaves" meant, in reality, to compensate the slave
owners. Ironically, the tweet suggests that generations of British taxpayers helped to end the slave trade (correctly said, slavery). I
would even argue that it thereby implicitly creates the illusion that
they actually helped the enslaved. In reality, their taxes were used
for a period of 180 years, apparently without their knowledge, to
pay off a loan that compensated slave owners rather than the enslaved. Obviously, the information as well as the language employed is misinterpreting and decontextualized the entire process
that ended slavery. Against the backdrop of the bank loan paid off
only in 2015, does slavery really belong to a distant past, with no
identifiable links to the present and therefore not being subject to

liability? Can this argument, prominently used in order to delegitimize reparations, be maintained? The Caribbean activists immediately raised these concerns after the tweet appeared and intervened into the public debate in a media conference they organized at the Centre for Reparation Research at the UWI on February 21, 2018.[16] Therein, they presented convincing points that deconstructed every single piece of information within the tweet. Moreover, they revisited again the compensation of slave owners, in particular its financial modalities, and provided new arguments in favor of reparations. I will summarize these arguments and further draw a conclusion, focusing on the arguments that directly answer to the dubiosity of the bank loan and the denial of British politics, but leaving out important arguments that counter the Western European premises of development assistance while denying responsibility for historical injustices.[17]

The most frequently used argument by British and other European governments is that slavery and the slave trade happened too long ago and therefore cannot be the subject of any form of political or legal settlement. Beckles dismantles this position as deceptive, false, duplicitous, and immoral, as the fact of repaying the bank loan until only two years ago makes it a "present-day activity" (Speech of Beckles at CRR media conference). Slavery is not as far away as European politicians wish to place it – neither for the people in the Caribbean nor for those in Great Britain. Beckles criticizes Cameron for his discourse of "let's move on" that systematically ignores the concerns of Caribbean societies and their people who still have to

---

16 "The CRR Media Conference on the British Treasury's Slavery Loans." (Centre for Reparation Research at the University of the West Indies 2018), http://www.reparationresearch.org/crr-media-conference-hm-trea sury-tweet-feb-21-2018/. The stream is placed into social media, the websites of CARICOM, Institute for Black World, and part of the discourses is quoted in Jamaican and international media. Among the panelists were Hilary Beckles, Verene Shepherd, Lord Anthony Gifford, and Minister Mike Henry – in this contribution I only quote Beckles.

17 I discuss this point more explicitly in Rauhut 2018a.

confront the harsh legacies of slavery and therefore cannot look at it as a closed chapter of the past. I would even say that he dismantles the hierarchy of international political relations, classifying the British government's position and Cameron's denial of recognition of historical injustice, by knowing about the loan and not admitting responsibility. Furthermore, Beckles underlines that abolition was not for a sense of morality, but rather for economic gains, as the slave owners profited economically in a double sense. In addition to cash money, they received a second form of compensation in the form of unpaid labor due to the "apprenticeship." Africans had to pay for their freedom – from that point he derives a legitimate right to get something back. I would furthermore add that the enslaved Africans and their descendants not only paid with labor, they paid by risking their own lives in the many rebellions and uprisings in order to fight slavery. The end of slavery first and foremost has to be attributed to Africans who fought for it and not to the British abolitionists alone. Finally, Beckles opposes the narrative that the British parliament abolished slavery or even 'helped to end slavery' by moral assumptions. He shifts the attention to the hard facts of economic calculation – the British planter aristocracy ensured their wealth by getting compensation in cash and labor. I would further add that the expression "help to end" stated in the tweet perpetuates once more the British abolition narrative that avoids any talk about the horrors of slavery and its legacies. But it was slavery that for a period of 300 years allowed a profitable enrichment based on the exploitation and dehumanization of millions of Africans and their descendants. The compensation records clearly show that this was not limited to the time of slavery but still continued in post-slavery periods.

We definitely could reason about a moral skepticism that must have been in the air in which many present taxpayers, and probably even some of those in the 1830s, would not have agreed to pay the slave-owners. This reflection finally leads to a serious moral doubt that many people share, then and now: Was it right to compensate the slave owners instead of the enslaved? British Historian Manjapra shows through contemporary press coverage of the 1820s that "many mainstream abolitionists felt uncomfortable about the compensation of slave-owners, but justified it as a pragmatic, if imperfect, way to achieve a worthy goal." Some were not only opposed to the idea, stating that "it would reconcile us to the crime," but they even suggested that it should be the enslaved instead of their owners who should get compensation (Manjapra, March 29, 2018). Finally, Draper points out that also the enslaved themselves expected reparations after the end of slavery:

> What the compensation process did not set out to do, of course, was to compensate the enslaved, or make any financial provision for the transition of the enslaved to freedom. The economic and social consequences for the enslaved of the structure adopted for the abolition of slavery were therefore disappointing relative to expectations prevalent ahead of Emancipation, and are arguably still evident in the former colonies of the West Indies and the Caribbean today. (Draper 2010, 271)

I would definitely confirm and expand on the reflections of Manjapra and Draper with my own empirical research in Jamaica. The analyses of my interviews conducted with the members of the Jamaican reparations council clearly uncover narratives about injustices done that not only refer to the crimes of slavery but also to the compensation of slave owners. Those narratives include the notion that justice is overdue, that people still expect to get something back and what they feel is owed to them (Rauhut forthcoming). Jamaican activists continue to work on the compensation records and new information on the bank loan in order to learn more empirical details. This includes not only the modalities of payments in the 1830s, but particularly the subsequent investments that planters, companies, insurances, banks, and churches undertook with that compensation money. Even more importantly, not only are they studying the systematic enrichment of the British elite, they put the spotlight on the other side of that wealth, on the impoverishment of those who remained in the Caribbean colonies without any compensation. The lasting legacies of slavery and non-compensation for the enslaved and their descendants encompass economic, social, political, juridical, cultural, racialized, and psychological dimensions that form the larger reparations framework.

According to the reparations activists, slavery-related problems have not been overcome by the formal end of slavery – they have persisted during colonialism and even after independence in the form of colonial-racialized social orders. These situations still produce inequalities, racial discrimination, and a lack of social mobility for people of African descent, who represent still the great majority of the Jamaican population. The activists argue that many of today's social and economic problems of the country have their origin, although not alone, in the compensation paid in the 1830s and therefore must be connected to that historical moment.

Countering the Arguments against Reparations

In order to illustrate the links between the past and the present, there have been calculations made of an equivalent to the £20 million paid as compensation to slave owners in 1834 of around £16.5 billion today.[18] This amount has not yet been claimed as a potential reparations sum, it rather serves as a symbolic argument in order to demonstrate the enormous wealth Great Britain extracted by unpaid enslaved labor and compensation.

It is up to economists to further quantify the material damage this has caused for the other side, the Caribbean former slave societies. In terms of non-material damage, my Jamaican interview partners have all underlined that it is impossible to quantify the many traumata slavery and compensation have caused and even more im-

---

18 Controversies about how to count appropriate parameters and methods are obvious. According to the various potential parameters applied (worth of cash money then and now, costs of unpaid labor, wealth extracted, economic investments etc.) different sums are circulating, spanning from £16.5 to £200 Billion, cf. for instance (Randall, February 26, 2013), the speech of Beckles at CRR media conference, or the booklet published by The Caricom Reparations Commission 2018.

possible to repair it by money. Furthermore, a simple monetary pay-out today would be contrary to their vision of reparations as a much more holistic process involving recognition, history, culture, and politics. They argue, however, that Great Britain could at least finance infrastructural investments in educational and health institutions, roads, houses, school reforms, the building of museums and research centers, as all these improvements require material resources. Reparations in this sense are sought as collective measures for the benefit of the whole society. In the case of Jamaica, as the great majority of population are descendants of the enslaved, these forms of infrastructural investments could be potentially perceived as true reparations. The obviously difficult "Realpolitik" of reparations (whenever it might come one day) is a relevant topic for another paper. This contribution primarily reflects upon why it is important for activists to calculate concrete amounts of money, however debatable they may be. They link the past to the present by symbolically relating the gains to the losses and consider this as necessary overall in order to counter the strong arguments against reparations. First, by investigating the compensation money of 1834 and where that money has gone in terms of subsequent development, they present an empirical research base that shows the long-term implications of unequal conditions through real facts and calculations. It shows the links between the compensation and rise of powerful British institutions still functioning today. Moreover, it relates the systematic enrichment of the British elite to a counter-rotating process that went on in the Caribbean colonies. The historical research deconstructs the assumption that slave owners and the enslaved were equal civilians after slavery ended. While the wealth of the British based on slavery and compensation was continuously passed from one generation to another, the descendants of the enslaved remained, for generations, disadvantaged in terms of accessing land, property, and capital for creating businesses and investment; many were still forced to work and live in conditions similar to slavery. This perspective highlights the entangled dimension of historical and ongoing global inequalities. In other words, both poverty and wealth have deep historical roots as they are structurally linked to slavery. When advocates scandalize uneven development between Europe and the Caribbean, evidenced by the compensation records, they implicitly appeal to accountability and moral-political responsibility. This can potentially deconstruct the dominant European position that all this happened too long ago, that it is impossible to quantify the damage and therefore impossible to repair the damage. Advocates argue instead that reparations are not generally impossible, as the wealth of Great Britain and by extension "the West" is traceable, similar to the impoverishment of the colonies.

On Shared Histories and Responsibilities:
Countering the Denial of Recognition

In conclusion, I will reflect on the impact of the research on the compensation records for potential reparations claims and how they finally contribute to academic and political debates on historical injustices. As my analysis of media discourses has demonstrated, Jamaican reparations activists deliberately use the compensation records in order to mobilize for a broader understanding that their slave-owning past is not over and that these legacies still shape the present in many forms. They insist on examining the legacies of a structurally unequal development that started by slavery and its causal relation to current global inequalities, but also the social injuries of a historical injustice that are still not acknowledged. The narratives about injustice include both the fact of slavery and particularly the compensation of British slave-owners in the 1830s and the consecutive systemic problems of the non-compensation for the enslaved people in the Caribbean. The compensation archives provide important sources that Jamaican advocates rely on in their public outreach activities and in their political campaigns for local and global audiences. They aim to win broader support for their claims and convince decision makers that Britain today owes the Caribbean some form of reparations. Moreover, in the light of the new research on the loan for compensation and the following political scandal, the whole process of abolition, emancipation, and freedom must be revised again. Caribbean activists dismantle the duplicity of the claim that 'it is too late to talk about slavery' when British taxpayers still had to back a loan related to slavery until 2015. Implicitly, they raise a challenging question: Is it really too late to repair the damages of the past? When it seems not too late to contribute to the enrichment of those who benefited from slavery and compensation? Activists scandalize the immorality of compensation and, moreover, they dismantle the immorality of British politics. The former Prime Minister David Cameron did know about the loan when he proposed to Jamaicans in 2015 that "we can move on," rejecting any conversation about slavery and compensation. It is the power of denial they lay open, knowing about the fact but not acting on it nor admitting political responsibility. By accusing Cameron (and all British governments before him) for their systematic denial of recognition of the injustices during and after slavery, despite knowing the facts, Jamaican activists strongly criticize the hierarchy of global power relations. At the same time, the activists expect to attract local and global support for their case by encouraging moral outrage in the people of the Caribbean and in Britain concerning paying back a highly disputable loan they didn't even know about, as well as the reaction to the double-faced position of the British Government.

The refusal of recognition of a historical injustice is finally in itself an epistemological problem: Who can assert, and from what position of power and geopolitical knowledge, that the past is over? For those who have to confront the legacies of slavery in their daily struggles with poverty, against the sense of being disadvantaged, still suffering from injustices that have not been acknowledged, those who have not had the privilege to profit for generations from an immoral accumulation of wealth – how can the past be over for these people? The systemic rejection of recognition, apology, and restorative measures not only attacks dignity, it increases harm in a way that people I have talked with feel: Have we no worth? Why are our concerns not taken seriously? I would argue that the denial of recognition in itself represents one of the strongest legacies of slavery. It is the power to not answer to the claims that affronts the descendants of the enslaved who have claimed reparations for generations in any region, beyond Jamaica and the Caribbean. The argument concerning living legacies seems to have been proven already before the scandal of the loan for compensation became public along with its magnitude in terms of time and money. They use this fact now to strengthen their position that slavery and economic exploitation do not belong to the past and still shape the present. They urge even more than before for holding an overdue conversation about the unequally shared burdens and profits of slavery and compensation between the Caribbean and Europe. By appealing to a moral duty to get something back, activists focus on the deep historical roots of structural inequalities and on the interrelations between poverty and wealth as a result of slavery. They further counter the duplicity of British politics that denies the recognition of historical injustice and neglects historical and political responsibility in relation to their former colonies in the Caribbean. They lastly urge the British government to take the concerns of Caribbean societies and its postcolonial governments more seriously and to establish a political relationship based on a more level playing ground. As academic activists, they clearly intervene into politics and counter the order of international power relations. Although this paper examines only Jamaica, the main argument that emphasizes the ongoing legacies of slavery and compensation in terms of global inequalities and political hierarchies is extensible to other (post)colonial relationships between Caribbean societies and the former colonizing countries of Europe. The framework of reparatory justice goes beyond the Anglophone Caribbean and should be discussed more consequently as a shared historical responsibility in European Politics.

Works Cited

Araujo, Ana L. 2017. *Reparations for Slavery and the Slave Trade. A Transnational and Comparative History*. London: Bloomsbury Academic.

Beckles, Hilary McDonald. 2013. *Britain's Black Debt: Reparations for Caribbean Slavery and Native Genocide*. Kingston: University of the West Indies Press.

Bilefsky, Dan. 2015. "David Cameron Grapples With Issues of Slavery Reparations in Jamaica." *The New York Times*, September 30, 2015. https://www.nytimes.com/2015/10/01/world/americas/david-cameron-grapples-with-issue-of-slavery-reparations-in-jamaica.html.

Butler, Kathleen M. 1995. *The Economics of Emancipation: Jamaica & Barbados, 1823-1843*. Chapel Hill: University of North Carolina Press.

Centre for Reparation Research at the University of the West Indies. 2018. "The CRR Media Conference on the British Treasury's Slavery Loans." http://www.reparationresearch.org/crr-media-conference-hm-treasury-tweet-feb-21-2018/.

Centre for the Study of the Legacies of British Slave-ownership. 2018. "Legacies of British Slave-ownership." https://www.ucl.ac.uk/lbs/.

Draper, Nicholas. 2010. *The Price of Emancipation: Slave-Ownership, Compensation and British Society at the End of Slavery*. Cambridge: Cambridge University Press.

Dunkley, Elaine. 2015. "David Cameron rules out slavery reparation during Jamaica visit." BBC, September 30, 2015. https://www.bbc.com/news/uk-34401412.

Government of the United Kingdom, Prime Minister's Office. 2015. "PM's speech to the Jamaican Parliament: David Cameron addressed the Jamaican Parliament during his visit to the region, praising the strong links between the UK and the Caribbean." News release, September 30. https://www.gov.uk/government/speeches/pms-speech-to-the-jamaican-parliament.

Hall, Catherine, Nicholas Draper, Keith MacClelland, Katie Do-
    nington, and Rachel Lang. 2014. *Legacies of British Slave-
    Ownership: Colonial Slavery and the Formation of Victorian
    Britain*. Cambridge: Cambridge University Press.

Hall, Catherine, Nicholas Draper, and Keith McClelland, eds. 2014.
    Emancipation and the Remaking of the British Imperial World.
    UCL/Neale series on British history. Manchester: Manchester
    University Press.

Hall, D. G. 1953. "The Apprenticeship Period in Jamaica, 1834-
    1838." *Caribbean Quarterly* 3.3: 142-166.

Higman, Barry W. 1976. *Slave Population and Economy in Jamai-
    ca, 1807-1834*. Cambridge: Cambridge University Press.

Jamaica Observer. 2015. "Britain has duty to clean up monumental
    mess of empire, Sir Hilary tells Cameron." *Jamaica Observer*,
    September 28. http://www.jamaicaobserver.com/news/Britain-
    has-duty-to-clean-up-monumental-mess-of-Empire--Sir-Hilary-
    tells-Cameron_19230957.

Journal of African American History, ed. 2018. "National and Inter-
    national Perspectives on Movements for Reparations." *Journal
    of African American History* 103 (Special issue): 1-2.

Manjapra, Kris. 2018. "When will Britain face up to its crimes
    against humanity? After the abolition of slavery, Britain paid
    millions in compensation – but every penny of it went to slave
    owners, and nothing to those they enslaved. We must stop over-
    looking the brutality of British history." *The Guardian*, March
    29.   https://www.theguardian.com/news/2018/mar/29/slavery-
    abolition-compensation-when-will-britain-face-up-to-its-crimes
    -against-humanity.

Randall, David. 2013. "Britain's Colonial Shame: Slave-Owners
    Given Huge Payouts After." *Independent*, February 26. https://
    www.independent.co.uk/news/uk/home-news/britains-colonial-
    shame-slave-owners-given-huge-payouts-after-abolition-85083
    58.html.

Rauhut, Claudia. 2018a. "Caribbean Activism for Slavery Repara-
    tions: an Overview." *Practices of Resistance in the Caribbean:*

Narratives, Aesthetics, Politics, ed. Wiebke Beushausen, Miriam Brandel, Joseph T. Farquharson, Marius Littschwager, Annika McPherson, and Julia Roth, 137-150. London, New York: Routledge.

———. 2018b. "Caribbean Leaders in the Transnational Struggle for Slavery Reparations." *Reshaping Glocal Dynamics of the Caribbean: Relaciones y Desconexiones – Relations et Déconnexions – Relations and Disconnections*, ed. Anja Bandau, Anne Brüske, and Natascha Ueckmann, 281-296. Heidelberg: Heidelberg University Publishing.

———. 2018c. "Mobilizing Transnational Agency for Slavery Reparations: The Case of Jamaica." *Journal of African American History* 103.1-2: 133-162.

———. Forthcoming. "On Redressing the Compensation of British Slave Owners in the 1830s as Basis for Caribbean Claims to Slavery Reparations."

Shepherd, Verene A. 1988. *Pens and Pen-keepers in a Plantation Society: Aspects of Jamaican Social and Economic History, 1740-1845*. Ph.D. Dissertation, unpublished, University of Cambridge.

———, Ahmed Reid, Cavell Francis, and Kameika Murphy. 2012. *Jamaica and the Debate over Reparation for Slavery: A Discussion Paper Prepared by the Jamaica National Bicentenary Committee*. Kingston: Pelican Publishers Limited.

The Caricom Reparations Commission. 2014. The Caricom Reparations Commission Ten Point Action Plan. http://caricomrepara tions.org/caricom/caricoms-10-point-reparation-plan/.

———. 2018. "Reparations for Native Genocide and Slavery: Reparation Booklet." http://www.reparationresearch.org/free-down loads/.

The Gleaner. 2015. "Reparation issue will cause greatest political movement if British PM fails to resolve, Beckles warns." *The Gleaner*, September 27. http://jamaica-gleaner.com/article/news/ 20150927/reparation-issue-will-cause-greatest-political-movement -if-british-pm-fails.

————. 2015. "PM raises reparation concern with David Cameron." *The Gleaner*, September 29. http://jamaica-gleaner.com/article/news/20150929/pm-raises-reparation-concern-david-cameron.

Wilmot, Swithin. 1984. "Not 'Full Free': The Ex-Slaves and the Apprenticeship System in Jamaica 1834-1838." *Jamaica Journal* 17: 3-10.

Memories in Displacement in the Public Space. The Monuments of Juana Azurduy and Christopher Columbus in Argentina[1]

CAROLINA CRESPO

Abstract

This paper analyzes temporalities, subjectivities, and political spatialities in conflict that were expressed through the discourses and images disseminated on the successive movements of the Christopher Columbus and Juana Azurduy monuments that took place in Buenos Aires from 2013 to 2017. I consider these movements of placement-displacement and re-placement of statues as metacultural performances that were constituted in memory devices with complex political implications. I discuss existing dichotomous positions on the policies of monumentalization and I examine what was sought to be fixed in these displacements with respect to the national imaginary of Argentina and the city of Buenos Aires. In particular, I unfold what was both visible and absent in order to show the displacement, tensions and/or sedimentation that, with respect to the indigenous, were expressed in these patrimonial policies of monumentalization promoted by different administrations of power and cultural hegemonies in dispute in Argentina.

In 2013, the president of Bolivia, Evo Morales, donated the statue of Juana Azurduy de Padilla to Argentina. Cristina Fernández de Kirchner,[2] president of Argentina at the time, disposed that it would be located where the monument of Christopher Columbus stood. The initiative to displace Columbus in favor of Juana generated a series

---

1   Translation from Spanish to English: Analía Kerman.
2   From now on, Evo and Cristina.

of controversies that made a great impact. Ortemberg (2016) and Premazzi (2015) examine certain aspects about it.[3] In 2017, two years
after its inauguration, the statue of Juana was finally displaced.

Since the nineteenth century, the location, aesthetics and orientation of monuments have been subject of discussion. In the new
millennium, these debates have re-emerged in different ways and
several governments in the Americas have commemorated new figures and/or eliminated others that had already been monumental-
ized. In this paper, I examine the conflicting temporalities, subjectivities, and political spatialities expressed in relation to the successive movements of these two monuments in Buenos Aires from
2013 to 2017. I discuss dichotomous visions about monumentalization policies and propose that such displacements must be seen as
metacultural performances created as memory devices of a complex
political potentiality.

Even though it may seem paradoxical, I examine what these
displacement performances sought to establish regarding not only a
national, but also a "*Porteño*," i.e, from the city of Buenos Aires,
imaginary. In particular, I unfold what was left in the order of the
visible and what remained obturated or absent to show the movements, tensions and/or sedimentations (Briones 2015) which, regarding the indigenous, were expressed in these policies of statues
driven movements by different power administrations and cultural
hegemonies in dispute in Argentina. For this analysis, I resort to
discourses and images observed in the public space and those reported in the media during the years in which these statues were
placed and displaced around different areas of the city.

---

3   Ortemberg (2016) analyzed the aesthetic, political and cultural senses of
    the statue of Juana Azurduy, how the work is integrated with the policies
    of Evo and Cristina, and its role in diplomacy. Premazzi (2015) exam-
    ined the disputes it aroused about national identity between 2013 and
    2014.

Layers of Time in Geography and of Geography in History

As part of cultural production, heritage state policies are articulated with the construction and regulation of a "desirable us" and the demarcation of those "we are not and do not want to be" in a process that involves conflicts and the unequal negotiation of memories, subjectivities, and a sense of place. This implies an active and dynamic process in which memories, forgetfulness, and silences are commemorated while producing physical and social places to cross and mediate sociocultural changes and political conflicts (Smith 2011, 42). Creating monuments has been one of the ways in which memories and concealments, presences and absences of physical and social places have been instituted in the daily public space to mediate changes and conflicts of a local, national, and international order. As Hite (2013) argues, through monuments, nations have projected an image of unity by commemorating victorious pasts, creating and venerating heroes, and omitting experiences of violence in order to create meaning about the past and space which mobilizes the present in relation to the current hegemonic project.

In Argentina, monuments acquired special relevance at the time of the first centenary in 1910. Faced with massive immigration and the existing heterogeneity, the economic-political and socio-cultural changes being promoted in the interest of creating cohesion, the monumentalization of male heroes and the appeal to a patriotic past in everyday practices, and the spaces, museums, schools, and celebrations were the paths taken to embody a national sentiment, affirm sovereignty and common citizenship (Bertoni 1992). That national feeling was configured while ignoring the contemporary indigenous peoples against whom Julio A. Roca had just waged the last military campaigns of extermination, expropriating their territory at the hands of the national state and subjugating those who were left alive while denying any Afro contribution and suspecting immigrants whose arrival in the nation had once been desired. In return, the Creole was vindicated as an identity figure through a discourse centered on the "melting pot" or the Hispanic-Indian model of mestization (Blache 1991-1992). This discourse became a political tool "to elaborate a homogenous image of the nation in which the indigenous gradually [should and] would disappear [to make a white and European nation] although, paradoxically, their marks became more and more evident" (Rodríguez 2008, 92).

Within the national framework, Buenos Aires became a locus of that "whiteness" and desired Europeanness. At the turn of the twentieth century, the aesthetics of this city were drawn to mirror European urbanization and promote the installation of monuments of heroes inspired by models of behavior and moral values associated with Western "civilization" (Gutiérrez Viñuales 2004). These monuments contributed as much to the processes of national and city communalization as to the establishment of international ties. Indeed, during the first centenary, several were part of rapprochement policies between national governments or migrant groups that acknowledged the welcome they had received by donating monuments. Among those monuments is that of Columbus, donated by the Italian community to commemorate the centenary and placed at a key location in the city.

The statue of Columbus responds to the prototype of classicism (Gutiérrez Viñuales 2004). It was built in white marble and stood on a pedestal behind the Government House. Its design, the *plaza*, and its orientation towards the sea, together with other features of urban landscape, have evoked and supported the notion of Europeanizing nationalist desire that feted the conquest of America under the euphemism of "discovery" and fueled the construction of the imaginary that we Argentines, and especially *Porteños*, "are white and descend from the ships."

In 2013, as part of a series of courtesies and bilateral agreements, Evo donated the statue of Juana Azurduy to Argentina and entrusted Argentine sculptor Zerneri with the work. Juana Azurduy was born in 1780 in Sucre, which is now in Bolivia. She fought with the Argentine army for the emancipation of America and was considered a heroine in the struggles to liberate "Upper Peru."[4] On tak-

---

4   "Upper Peru" (Spanish: *Alto Perú*) is a name for the land that was governed by the Real Audiencia of Charcas. It comprised a large part of the current territory of Bolivia and the south of Peru.

ing office, Cristina began to bring Juana out of the shadows, naming her in speeches as a heroine of the Independence of America, recovering her image through its reproduction in paintings and banknotes, promoting her to General of the Argentine Army and naming gender policies and a gas pipeline with Bolivia after her. At the same time, her history was disseminated in magazines and children's programs on public digital television and in the Historical Review Institute, created during her administration.

The decision to place the monument where the statue of Columbus stood must be read in terms of an international process in which, as I mentioned, symbols and statues are being reviewed, discussed and/or removed. By way of example, in Venezuela, President Chávez had the statue of Columbus removed in 2004, citing his genocidal character; in 2012, a debate began in the U.S.A. regarding the commemorative statues of the Confederate movement that have been taken down in certain states; and in 2000, Chile created the statue of Salvador Allende. However, this must also be seen as continuation of a gesture and a form of commemoration inaugurated during Néstor Kirchner's administration with the removal of the pictures of the 1976-1983 military dictators that marked the incorporation of the struggle for memory and human rights as a state policy. Furthermore, it should be observed as a product of Cristina Kirchner's concern to correlate national and Latin American politics and history within the framework of the bicentennial; it is also to vindicate the role of women in the struggle under a certain discursive imprint and the most adversative government that characterized her administration (Raiter 2013).[5] In this context, the performance of displacements and replacements of symbols became a memory

---

5   Museums, cultural centers, and the Memory and Human Rights Space
     were created. The Siqueiros mural was restored. The image of Eva Perón
     appeared on the Ministry of Social Development building and she was
     declared "Woman of the Bicentennial." The statues of Father Carlos
     Mugica and Arturo Jauretche were unveiled. Lounges at House of Government dedicated to women, Latin American patriots, native peoples,
     etc. were opened (Sarmiento 2016).

device with political implications. In 2012, banknotes of the highest value were issued with the figure of Eva Perón in place of Julio A. Roca.[6] In 2014, former president Sarmiento was replaced by the commemoration of the Falklands War on the 50 peso bill and Juana Azurduy was added to Manuel Belgrano on the 10 peso bill. Likewise, the content and accent afforded to the October 12th holiday was also modified. Since 2010, it has been known as "Diversity Day" as opposed to "Race Day" and, in 2014, the Indigenous Peoples' Hall, previously called Christopher Columbus Hall, was inaugurated in Government House.

Shortly after the donation was made public, the press published images of a company working on the Columbus monument and informed that it would be sent to Mar del Plata, 400 km from the city of Buenos Aires, and the statue of Juana Azurduy would be put in its place. The newspapers attributed the idea behind its displacement to Venezuelan President Hugo Chávez. The images of the pedestal surrounded by scaffolding and a crane carrying the statue that were seen in the square and circulated in the media unleashed a series of conflicts. The statue had suffered certain deterioration due to erosion and acts of violence including the bombing of Plaza de Mayo in 1955 to oust President Perón and a bomb that exploded at its base in 1987 during Alfonsín's administration. Government spokespeople reported that they had hired a company to restore the monument but the power of the images accompanying the news of the relocation of the monument had a strong impact on public opinion.

For those positions that maintain that there is nothing more invisible than the permanent and daily visibility of the monument (Persino 2008), it is worth noting an opposite example. There were mobilizations, parliamentary debates, political speeches, reflections on history, and numerous press reports in which journalists, law-

6   Some news items speculated that Roca would be replaced by Juana Azurduy. A legislative project relaunched this initiative proposed by those who wished to demonumentalize Roca, but the executive decided to replace him with Evita.

yers, anthropologists, historians, restorers, etc. intervened. The news conceptualized the phenomenon using the metaphor of "battle." They defined it as a cultural, historical as well as judicial and jurisdictional battle:

> "The decision put the country's Italian community *on a warpath.*" (*Diario Popular*, May 31, 2013)

> "Reflections on the Christopher Columbus/Juana Azurduy *'cultural'* battle." (*La política* online, June 5, 2013)

> "A *fight* arose between City and Nation, plus a judicial battle." (*Clarín*, December 17, 2013)[7]

In all cases, regardless of those who supported the measure or those who opposed it, the transfer decision was defined as a "replacement": either Colón or Azurduy. Those who opposed it saw the replacement as the destruction of symbolism, culture, and history.

Two NGOs involved with the city's heritage and various Italian community associations filed appeals for protection and precautionary measures that prevented movement on the question of the monument for almost two years. Irrespective of the history of Columbus as a figure, they appealed for the history of the monument and respect and preservation of the heritage of the city by making a significant differentiation between the "inherited" (Columbus) and the "new" (Azurduy). They argued especially on the subject of rights: the right to decide on space, heritage, history, identity, and, particularly, the right to exercise a change in all these dimensions. Given the government of the city of Buenos Aires, at that time in the hands of Mauricio Macri, who belonged to a conservative and neoliberal oligarchy and was the main opponent of the national government, a jurisdictional conflict arose over the monument and the square. Until an agreement was reached in 2014, control over the monument expressed a partisan and cultural policy contest.

---

7   Emphasis by author.

For two years, the media repeatedly showed images of Columbus being towed or lying on the floor facing upwards (see Figure 1) with parts scattered around the square, as if they were his ruins or remains. This led it to his detractors defining it as an act of sacrilege, irrationality, and presidential authoritarianism, even hinting at the destruction of the monument, no longer at its replacement, as terrorism or "K Talibanism."[8] They discussed who had the power to decide on the monuments that were to be removed, but symptomatically failed to discuss who had the power to decide on those that were installed. At the same time, these images were understood positively by those who supported the project, as a constructive fact that redefined the collective memory. As anthropologist Masotta wrote in one newspaper, it was like "an eloquent image of the transition of a society that evaluates where to deposit its traumatic pasts and where to direct its future gaze" (*Página 12*, July 24, 2013).

Figure 1. Image of the Columbus statue lying on the floor face up, 2013-2015.[9]

---

8   Kirchnerism is locally designated with the letter "K."

9   https://es.wikipedia.org/wiki/Monumento_a_Cristóbal_Colón_(Buenos _Aires)#/media/Archivo:Estatua_de_Cristóbal_Colón_en_proceso_de_ restauración_-_Buenos_Aires.jpg.

On Movements, Detentions, and Tensions

Which layers of history, subjectivities, and territorialities are expressed, constructed, and addressed when discussing a monument? Which ones drive the images of their displacement? Those who defended the permanence of the statue of Columbus proposed communicating the contradictory historical times and symbols by placing both statues in the same or different spaces in the city. The focus of discussion was not so much the incorporation of Juana into the city but rather her replacing Columbus and those who decided it. The defense of "coexistence" was based on a longstanding vision of national identity centered, as I pointed out, on the Hispanic-Indian blend or a relativism that has only recently recognized diversity, but not conquest and asymmetry. They also justified it by affirming the "inevitability" of the "discovery," differentiating Columbus from Cortés or Pizarro, and expressing a "necessary" relationship between the Enlightenment and the American Revolution. Some even distinguished the "discovery" of America that associated Columbus, modernity, and the extension of knowledge from the "conquest," attributing it to a later period linked to indigenous genocide. Hence they criticized the replacement, because they believed it changed national history and that of humanity, and they associated these modifications with the destruction of the monument, *ergo*, of the symbol.

Conversely, those who supported the displacement of the statue made a critical reflection on history. They saw it as a powerful and challenging political gesture that invited thinking on what was silenced or absent in the visible and daily presence of monuments that are almost 100 years old.[10] They considered Columbus to represent the subjugation of America and recalled his ideas and actions of domination as the beginning of the extermination of the indigenous peoples on the continent. They linked the colonialism of the Spanish

---

10   These proposals are aligned with discussions generated by the "anti-monumentalist" movement that emerged around 1970 in Germany.

conquest with the republic and recalled that official history had rendered the participation of women and indigenous peoples invisible in the struggles for the emancipation of America.

The indigenous reference figures made divergent positions public. Since 2010, a series of disagreements have arisen within indigenous leadership on the question of the government (Briones 2015). These differences extended to the debates on the movement of the monuments. Those who supported the government claimed it was part of a decolonization policy. They mobilized with posters that read "Yes to decolonization," "Bye Columbus," and "Columbus [Nunca Más] Never Again!" – a phrase used to repudiate the state terrorism of the last military dictatorship but now referring to Columbus as symbol of the genocide and ethnocide of indigenous peoples. They described the importance of reflecting on the history of the conquest of America. They recalled the hegemony of the "liberal, subservient" project of the centenary that prevailed with its story and symbolism, justifying massacres, expropriations, and the indigenous colonization of a "white and europeanized" nation. They correlated this project with Macri while celebrating the recovery of the "Patria Grande"[11] of the Kirchner administration, and identified indigenous and non-indigenous people who fought for the emancipation of the continent as "genuine libertarian leaders." They considered the removal of pictures of the genocidal military in the same vein as the displacement of the statue of Columbus. They supported the visibility of women's struggle for independence and pointed to Juana as a revolutionary who recalled the participation of indigenous people and Afro-descendants in the struggles for American freedom.

---

11 "Patria Grande" was a political concept that synthetized a project conceived by the South American liberators. It was referred to the political unification of the Hispano-American nations. During the Kirchner government, it was claimed under the project of a regional integration, e.g., Unasur, Mercosur.

The displacement of Columbus for Juana was defined as the de-monumentalization of Columbus as a symbol. The State was understood to have incorporated a policy of remembrance whose initiative came from historically subalternized and alternized sectors. These groups considered important not to eliminate monuments – because this could foster social forgetfulness – rather than keeping alive a critical memory of the past through their displacement and replacement. This reignited previous debates regarding what to do with spaces and symbols linked to torture during the last military dictatorship and those related to the statues of people who were responsible for genocide, such as Roca and Juan de Garay.[12] Debates that led some indigenous and non-indigenous people to demonumentalize the first and to protest at the statue of the latter.

The institutional incorporation of certain "popular" demands within the government of the state was one of the forms of governmentality promoted by the Kirchner administration. History and heritage did not escape this and the emerging images of the transfer of statuary symbols by the government were powerful in that regard. However, even institutionalizing subordinated ways of challenging official history, the proposal propelled another course in which the revision of relations with indigenous peoples did not take center stage in the presidential discourse. "Decolonization" aimed to highlight the role of women in the struggle, connecting Juana's struggle with that of the Mothers of the Plaza de Mayo (Ortemberg 2016), defining her as a *mestiza* and enhancing the emancipation of a popular and Latin American nation. However, the gruesome events of extermination, violence, subordination, and indigenous agency, which were directly linked to those symbols, did not enter the presidential discussion. This paradox revealed the limits in the languages and changing accents that this process of hegemony, defined as national-popular, was setting. The occlusion of these facts and subjects corresponded to a continuous history of subalternization within the framework of a political present anchored in a "national-popu-

---

12   The official story considered Garay the second founder of Buenos Aires.

lar" matrix that proposed an ambivalent response to the indigenous claims that could obstruct the political and economic interests of capital.[13]

In 2015, national and city officials agreed to transfer Columbus to the Costanera, and the statue of Juana Azurduy was inaugurated. This became a diplomatic event and involved economic and political cooperation agreements between Bolivia and Argentina. Juana emerged in a place of power within the urban landscape, facing towards the Women's Hall of the Bicentennial of the House of Government and, unlike Columbus, with her eyes on the continent. Among the tallest statues in the country, it was designed in bronze and sat on a pyramidal base inspired by the Tiahuanaco culture, in line with the statue of Manuel Belgrano, a hero who fought for independence. At Evo's request, she was depicted in movement and as a protector. She is in battle with a sword in her left hand to symbolize not war but liberation, and her right hand is extended to protect the boy and the town. She holds a baby with an *aguayo*[14] and twelve small figures around her represent different indigenous peoples. The statue breaks with the previous heroic aesthetic that existed in Buenos Aires and was limited to individual white male figures. Paradoxically it shows the indigenous person who had been absent from the presidential discourse and underexposed in the appeal to miscegenation attributed to Juana and the national and regional history. Ortemberg claims that Zerneri combined a narrative of historical tension "between the values of miscegenation of the heroine and the visibility of ethnic specificities and the rights of indigenous peoples" (Ortemberg 2016, 108). I wonder if that tension

---

13   Although indigenous people were incorporated in state institutions, their becoming was shown in Government House hall and a survey on the indigenous territory started; evictions and repressions were silenced in some provinces and territorial titling was not resolved nor other claims heard, especially those that contravened neo-extractivist policies.

14   Translator's note: An *aguayo* is a rectangular garment particularly worn by indigenous women in Argentina, Bolivia, Peru, and northern Chile as a backpack, coat, or adornment.

did not prevail also in the presidential discourse that, as Briones points out, modified "the way of telling national and regional history, claiming images of a mestizo nation that – even in a racialized way – allows for the contribution of the indigenous peoples in its constitution" (Briones 2015, 41).

After signing the agreements and the speeches made by each president in the *Casa Rosada*,[15] the inauguration was followed by a celebration in which members of the Bolivian community in Argentina and other indigenous guests participated.[16] At the celebration, the value of independence and commitment "in the construction of the *Patria Grande*, Free and Sovereign" was vindicated. Juana's "patriotic and heroic struggle" was recalled, feeding into "the independence of both nations and giving birth to Latin American fraternity and integration." The monument was considered to be a reminder "of the commitment shown in the struggle for the liberation of the peoples." Evo exalted Juana as a "guerrilla fighter for independence" and affirmed "we live in times of liberation." The event continued with a dinner which saw the participation of officials from each country, the sculptor, and the Mothers and Grandmothers of Plaza de Mayo. The speeches made by both heads of state referred to inclusive and redistributive agenda of each administration, recalled recent episodes of solidarity in economic and political matters, and stressed the need to be partners in achieving regional economic integration. Evo defined the event as a form of decolonization and highlighted the political project of Latin American integration and inclusion of "the most abandoned and forgotten sectors of history." Cristina emphasized the policy of inclusion of the most vulnerable and middle class sectors of her government and evoked the role of women in liberation struggles.

Several indigenous reference figures were not opposed to the decision to displace and replace the monuments, but reactive to what

---

15   This is the local name for the Government House.

16   Although very numerous, the Bolivian community had not expressed itself in the debate.

they saw as political rhetoric. They denounced the national government's silencing of the discrimination and dispossession of indigenous territories claimed by communities in several provinces. They
denounced the erosion of their rights and territories by neo-extrac-
tive capital. On the symbolic level, they added that the indigenous
origin of Juana Azurduy had been denied and that, by rescuing her as
a Bolivian or a heroine from "Upper Peru," a discourse of miscegenation was recovered to refer to that aspect of identification in which
the indigenous person appeared to fade away as a spectral figure. As
the statue of Juana was inaugurated, the indigenous "*QoPiWiNi*"
group from Formosa had been camping out in Buenos Aires for five
months without being heard. They denounced abuses carried out in
their province. Those who had mounted the camp called for a march
to the monument under the slogan "Thank you, Juana Azurduy" to
deliver a letter listing their claims to Evo, although in the end it
could not be delivered. Months later, in my fieldwork, I heard Mapuche people who had been invited to the inauguration complaining
that they had only been allowed to see the celebration behind the
barriers surrounding the event.

In 2017, the statue of Juana Azurduy was itself displaced. Its
pyramidal base was removed to stand at a lower height opposite the
Centro Cultural Kirchner (see Figure 2).[17] Since the end of 2015, as
part of the "move to the right" emerging in several countries of the
American continent, Mauricio Macri won the presidency in a party
alliance representing a conservative and neoliberal project. The government decided to create what is known as "*Paseo del Bajo.*" This
project included the construction of a heliport in the square where
the statue had been located, increasing green spaces and carrying

---

17   This cultural center functions in the former *Correo Argentino* (Argentine
     Post) building. The postal system was privatized and awarded to the
     Macri group in the 1990s. In 2001, given the company's debts to the
     State, a lawsuit was instigated, although no final ruling has been an-
     nounced yet. During the Kirchner government, the building returned to
     State ownership and it was restored as a cultural center. Its name has
     been the cause of discussions ever since Macri came to power.

out roadworks changes that would "improve" traffic flows by connecting highways. More than looking at the past, they claimed these
changes were "looking to the future." The *Paseo del Bajo* project
involved moving the "Tree of Guernica" and the statue of Juan de
Garay, a monument by which an indigenous community usually
congregates to denounce his acts of genocide. The displacement of
Juan de Garay was described by the government as a form of enhancing both his figure and that of Juana Azurduy as a way of reap-
praising the *Centro Cultural Kirchner*, an iconic symbol of a longstanding dispute. Its relocation is linked to a series of gestures and
new strategies employed by the neoliberal oligarchy in Argentina.
As soon as he became president, Macri also resorted to the displacement of symbols, although he gave the performance a particular
twist. He removed several pictures of pro-independence leaders
from the *Casa Rosada*, including Juana Azurduy and Manuel Belgrano. He organized the celebration of the Bicentennial of Independence by inviting the King of Spain and the Presidents of Italy,
Paraguay, and Chile, ignoring Evo Morales.[18] He replaced the his-
torical-political symbols on banknotes with the quasi-extinct local
fauna of different regions of the country. Government officials justified him in the desire to make an impact on life, raise awareness on
the environment, and appeal to federalism. Beyond the paradox, in
the context of a public policy zealously promoted by neo-extractivist capitalism, it represents the measures that have been part of a
strategy of "emptying" all "discussion" about the past and politics
which they claim becomes a conflict[19]; replacing culture with na-

---

18   Its absence was significant because in the Congress of Tucumán, people
     from "Upper Peru" were represented and are now part of the Pluri-
     national State of Bolivia. It was also symptomatic that in his speech
     Macri attributed a feeling of anguish to the patriots for separating from
     Spain.

19   The trials for crimes against humanity were slowed down, funds were
     reduced to spaces of memory, the Supreme Court cut the sentence of a
     repressor of the dictatorship, the history of the last dictatorship was trivi-
     alized, etc. Although it was not finally implemented, when Macri was

ture, history with space, the past with the future. Without going any further, the relocation of Juana Azurduy was not justified by reflecting on the history, culture and monumentalization of heroes, but on what this change would bring to the spatial future of the city: no longer looking backwards but forwards; no longer reviewing the "conflict" and appealing to the "struggle" as the engine of politics but exhibiting the "possibility of dialogue" between opposites – the communication pillar of the new government's policy – proclaimed by those who had criticized the fact that the Columbus statue had been replaced by the figure of Juana, e.g., NGOs, Italian community, journalists.

While certain demands for the return of Columbus to the area behind the *Casa Rosada* continued, the transfer of Juana Azurduy generated no mobilization, not even by patrimonialist NGOs that had questioned the displacement of Columbus and other monuments in the city from a "protectionist" view of heritage. Only a few voices were raised in various means of communication, including one that urged us to remember that "the geography of the city is ideological and the location of its monuments is a particular narrative of History. It is a story that comes and goes, that does not know where to place its women because the story was always told by men (i.e., the monuments)" ("Nothing shakes us," *Página 12*, June 2, 2017).

The lack of public debate on this movement that redefined space and time in a regime with dominance in the future and in the "coexistence" of opposites should not be read as a newly reached consensus. Zerneri interpreted the transfer of the statue as a political issue, even believing that at its new location it would be more appreciated because the area behind the *Casa Rosada* had been closed to the public for years.

The transfer of the monument was filmed and photographed in different media but was not accompanied by any official discourse reviewing the history or highlighting the controversy that had led to

---

governor of the city of Buenos Aires in 2013, he proposed to remove history as a subject in the last years of high school.

the movement of the monuments. Conceived under the idea of heritage as a "thing" or as materiality, both statues were projected in the space from an aesthetic perspective as equally valid "objects," purged of their senses. The most conservative newspaper, which had reviled the displacement and replacement of Columbus, now naturalized the transfer as part of the relocation of monuments that usually occurs in a developing city. Two images accompanied the scarce news about the event: the holes in the statue of Juana and the video of its transfer. Is it an attempt to symbolize the deterioration and the defeat of a project of a nation and of Latin American integration at the hands of another that replicates the colonial legacy? Is it the foreshadowing of a change in policy regarding issues of "order" in which the claims and struggles of certain sectors against a system that oppresses them will find a response based on stigmatization, legal prosecution, repression, and death? If the government started its mandate with the symbolic gesture of accompanying those indigenous people who had not been heard, the year in which Juana was moved from her place saw a fierce repression of the Mapuche communities that had gone to recover their territory.[20]

While Columbus today stands facing the River Plate on a pedestal on the Costanera, Juana is in profile to Government House, without her pyramidal base. Hardly raised on a marble block that westernizes her figure and far from Government House, she cannot be seen from its halls, nor can she look inside (see Figure 3). She can only observe at a distance the place of power that she was able to occupy for a brief period.

---

20 Repression led to the death of a Mapuche and the forced disappearance of a young man who had gone to support the claims, who was later found dead. Since then, Mapuches have been overexposed in the news under old and new stigmas and many have been legally prosecuted.

Figure 2. Juana Azurduy's monument stand in front of the *Centro Cultural Kirchner* without her pyramidal base. 2018. Photo by Carolina Crespo.

Figure 3. Juana Azurduy's monument raised on a marble block. 2019. Photo by Carolina Crespo.

Final Words

Unlike other countries of the continent, where the revision of past figures, from which national and city identities were modeled, led to

the elimination of their monumentalization, e.g., Columbus in Venezuela and Los Angeles; Che Guevara in Paraiba under Jair Bolsonaro's current administration; the statues of the Confederate movement in certain U.S. cities, despite Donald Trump's opposition,[21] in
Argentina, the review of memory operated through another type of
device, not the suppression of the monument but the effects of
meaning that caused its displacements from and replacements in
places of power. In this framework, certain dichotomies that have
accompanied reflections on monumentalization policies need to be
nuanced. I refer to those that interrelate statuary fixity with invisi-
bility, and those that attribute monument immobility with perpetua-
tion of the statu quo and mobility as a challenge to established power.
Not only has the displacement of these monuments been a memory
device used by the neoliberal oligarchy in Argentina for the purpose
of restoring the "order" and its place in power, but these policies are
also a metaphor for the movements, tensions, and sedimentations
operating within each hegemonic project of recent years.

The monumentalization of Juana Azurduy was accompanied by
a series of complex operations: replacing Columbus and moving
him away from the space and the history of power. The movement
challenged canons that were believed to be immutable in the imagination of the "national community" and the *Porteña* community: the
space of women within a geography forbidden by men; the mestizo
over the white; Latin America over Europe; and the exhortation of
struggles and confrontation to achieve emancipation. The gesture of
Cristina's government formed part of a policy of memory and space
which, with the displacement of Columbus and his images, located
those past and "uncomfortable" geographies that were celebrated
and crystallized in undisputed heritage symbols, national policies,
and international geopolitics. In parallel, it venerated other stories
and hidden spaces. The history of Argentina and Buenos Aires had

---

21   The cases show the impossibility of generalizing and establishing a line-
     ar correlation between current "right-wing" governments and the elimi-
     nation of "monumentalized" figures.

not recognized Juana Azurduy and looked very little at "Upper Peru." But the lack of centrality of the indigenous peoples in this and
other government policies prevented consensus building on a history that has so far remained on the margins of the accountable in the
regimes of state memory; paraphrasing Briones (2015, 24), this expresses how sedimented some visions continue to be even when re-
articulated in and from other styles of constructing hegemony.

Meanwhile, the new government continued with this memorial
performance but only to produce an inverse effect. The displacement of the statue of Juana Azurduy in 2017, not its elimination, has
been combined with masked attempts to interrupt the question about
disruptive pasts, to close the review of colonial experiences, "clear"
certain political ideas of daily spaces, and make evident the exercise
of a power that locates not confrontations or struggles, but the con-
vivial dialog of opposites at the center of its State policy. A dialog
that equals the unequaled on the basis of the interest of restoring the
"order" of a white western oligarchy, centered on "progress." As
Richard (2019) suggests, neoliberalism (especially that emerging
post "national-popular" governments) is not only an economic doctrine, nor a set of governance techniques. It is a way of fabricating
docile subjectivities, less through going without languages and signs
to which it is opposed, than its circulation under forms emptied of
content or redemptive inscription. In 2018, the president stated that
the relationship with the European Union was natural because in
South America we are all descendants of Europeans, and he rejected
a Latin American integration policy like that favored by the previous government. Regarding indigenous policies, he incorporated a
historical demand of these peoples, to include them in the area of
human rights, and he met with indigenous people who had not been
previously heard, although he continues to ignore demands for territorial rights. In fact, the responses to certain indigenous territorial
claims have been repression, death, stigmatization, and criminal prosecution as terrorists. The continued existence of the statue of Juana
Azurduy, albeit displaced from a space of power in the city, is a reminder that whiteness and masculinity have returned to the center of

city and national power. But even so, its permanence expresses the tensions and struggles to challenge the veneration of an urban, national, white, and masculine space, alongside the impossibility of ignoring the role of women and the limits of the rhetoric of indigenous diversity in contexts of neoliberalism.

Works Cited

Bertoni, Liliana. 1992. "Construir la nacionalidad: Héroes, estatuas y fiestas patrias 1887-1891." *Boletín del Instituto de Historia Argentina y Americana Dr. Ravignani* 5: 77-111.

Blache, Martha. 1991-1992. "Folklore y nacionalismo en la Argentina. Su vinculación de origen y su desvinculación actual." *Runa. Archivos para las Ciencias del Hombre* 20: 69-89.

Briones, Claudia. 2015. "Políticas indigenistas en Argentina: entre la hegemonía neoliberal de los años noventa y la 'nacional y popular' de la ultima decada." *Antípoda* 21: 21-48.

Gutiérrez Viñuales, Rodrigo. 2004. *Monumento conmemorativo y espacio público en Iberoamérica.* https://www.ugr.es/~rgutierr/PDF2/LIB%20011.pdf.

Hite, Katherine. 2013. *Política y arte de la conmemoración. Memoriales en América Latina y España.* Santiago de Chile: Mandrágora.

Ortemberg, Pablo. 2016. "Monumentos, memorialización y espacio público: reflexiones a propósito de la escultura de Juana Azurduy." *Tarea* 3.3: 96-125.

Persino, María Silvina. 2008. "Memoriales, museos, monumentos: La Articulación de una memoria pública en la Argentina Posdictatorial." *Revista Iberoamericana* 74.222: 1-16.

Premazzi, Ana. 2015. *¿COLON versus JUANA AZURDUY? La pelea por los símbolos y la identidad nacional en el kirchnerismo.* Tesis de Licenciatura en Ciencias Antropológicas, Facultad de Filosofía y Letras, Universidad de Buenos Aires.

http://antropologia.filo.uba.ar/sites/antropologia.filo.uba.ar/files
/documentos/Premazzi%20-%20Tesis.pdf.
Raiter, Alejandro. 2013. "Capítulo 5. ¿Existe una lógica discursiva
kirchnerista? Constancias y alternancias." *Discurso, política y
acumulación en el kirchnerismo*, vol. 7, ed. Javier Balsa, 105-
141. Buenos Aires: Centro Cultural de la Cooperación Floreal
Gorini/Universidad Nacional de Quilmes.
Richard, Nelly. 2019. "Debate Panel 2." Paper presented in the
Coloquio Internacional "La memoria en la encrucijada del pre-
sente: El problema de la justicia." Centro Cultural Haroldo
Conti, Buenos Aires, April 10-12. https://www.youtube.com/
watch?v=rB3nEuJB-pU&list=PL_ZbR9W0L2nutSB7NzMRvs
5aDIHJe-6EF&index=4&t=0s .
Rodríguez, Lorena. 2008. "Mestizos o indios puros? El Valle Cal-
chaquí y los primeros antropólogos." *Revista Avá* 13: 77-92.
Sarmiento, Gabriel. 2016. "Políticas visuales de la memoria en Argentina en el período kirchnerista (2003-2015)." https://www.
academia.edu/26372089/Politicas_visuales_de_la_memoria_en
_Argentina_en_el_período_kirchnerista_2003-2015.
Smith, Laurajane. 2011. "El 'espejo patrimonial'. ¿Ilusión narcisista
o reflexiones múltiples?" *Antípoda* 12: 39-63.

Populism and the Imagination of the Past and Future

PAULA DIEHL

Abstract

The current essay elaborates on the relationship between populism and democracy by focusing on the political imaginary. It reflects the emancipation that was made possible by the democratic imaginary and the contradictions that were raised by it. Reflecting these contradictions helps to understand not just the intrinsic potential for crisis within democracy, but equally its development into a major crisis when social, economic, political, and cultural uncertainties increase. The paper will explore the chances and risks of populism for democracy by taking the two temporalities of the democratic imaginary into account. The main argument is that populism modifies the democratic imaginary by merging its two dimensions and by eclipsing their contradictions. Finally, the text evaluates the chances and risks of populism for the democratic imagination of the future.

Introduction

Modern democratic societies are contradictory societies. They are grounded on normative premises which are not fully realized in practice. Contradictions of Western[1] democracies are well known. They manifest themselves especially when it comes to the distribution of rights, to the representation of minorities, to the implementa-

---

1   This article acknowledges that the modern concept of democracy is a Western one issued by the American and French Revolutions. Latin America embraced this notion of democracy, which until now continues to provide a normative horizon to politics. In times of dictatorship, dictatorial regimes used the term in order to blame communists and the left for not being democratic.

tion of civil rights, and to the transfer of the exercise of sovereignty to political representatives. The current essay proposes to understand these contradictions as a product of different temporalities within the democratic imaginary. The first temporality sets a horizon that allows society to imagine the future in terms of an emancipatory space. This dimension of the democratic imaginary can be depicted as the normative foundation of democracy. The second temporality of the democratic imaginary is connected to social and political norms on the level of their realization in political and social practices. However, these two dimensions do not necessarily evolve in the same manner and in the same speed, creating an intrinsic contradiction within democracy. They have two different temporalities.

Such contradictions are easily detectable when it comes to the political representation of the people. In the foundational dimension of the democratic imaginary, popular sovereignty is presupposed as a core element of democracy, as its symbolic matrix (Lefort 1988a).

Yet, when it comes to the implementation of democratic government, popular sovereignty suffers a transformation: it becomes an object of representation. On the practical level, the people do not govern but their representatives do, creating a tension between popular sovereignty and political representation. Pierre Rosanvallon formulates this tension in terms of aporias of modern emancipation (Rosanvallon 2006, 199). This is the reason why crisis is intrinsic to representative democracy. Precisely at this point, populism arises and promises to bring the power back to the people. It sets an imagination of democracy that negates its contradictions by drawing a picture of a harmonious society as a place where the people can have their power back. The imagination of the sovereign people would be a perfect picture of direct democracy if populist leaders would not present themselves as the voice of the people and simultaneously pretend to lead them.

The current essay elaborates on the relationship between populism and democracy by focusing on the political imaginary. It reflects the emancipation that was made possible by the democratic imaginary and contradictions that were raised by it. Reflecting these contradictions helps to understand not just the intrinsic potential for crisis within democracy, but equally its development into a major crisis when social, economic, political, and cultural uncertainties increase. The paper will explore the chances and risks of populism for democracy by taking the two temporalities of the democratic imaginary into account. The main argument is that populism modifies the democratic imaginary by merging its two dimensions and eclipsing their contradictions. Finally, the text evaluates the chances and risks of populism for the democratic imagination of the future.

Democracy and Emancipation

Modern democracy can be regarded in different ways: as a procedure to choose the government, a political regime, and as a form of society. When one says democracy, different concepts come to mind. I think democracy needs to be considered in its complexity and all the three dimensions mentioned above must be considered. In order to understand the phenomenon of populism and its consequences, it is necessary to face democracy from the perspective of the political imaginary. The argument for this choice is that the political is deeply dependent on the way a society imagines itself. Following Claude Lefort (1988a) and Cornelius Castoriadis (1987), I argue that instituting society and establishing a political order are both mechanisms, which are only possible because the social and the political are objects of social imagination. If the choice is to define democracy in a complex way, as is the case in the current essay, starting from the political imaginary allows to see what makes the political, political order, and political institutions in democracy possible and how populism affects the imagination of democracy. Understanding democracy means also understanding the constitution and transformation of the political imaginary. However, there is another important theoretical choice here: Populism is not defined as a category regarding political actors, but as a political logic that varies in intensity and can affect the imagination of democracy in different degrees. These two theoretical and methodological choices open the perspective for the importance of symbolic representation involved in the constitution of the very first step in the transformation of democratic society: its imagination.

The political is deeply connected with the imaginary, and the imaginary changes historically and culturally. Modern democracy is a magnificent example of these changes and is inconceivable without the historical experience of the revolutions of the eighteenth century. One of its most important innovations is that modern democracy sets free the possibility of imagining the future in terms of autonomy and emancipation. Castoriadis reflects autonomy in terms of praxis and project, which are both part of the modern revolutionary imagination. "There is an internal relation between what is intended (the development of autonomy) and that through which it is intended (the exercise of this autonomy). These are two moments of a single process" (Castoriadis 1987, 49).

According to Lefort, the French Revolution was able to establish a new imagination of society and give birth to the modern project of emancipation. For Lefort,

> the political character of the Revolution becomes perceptible only if we grasp, on the one hand, the signs of the imaginary elaboration by virtue of which social relations are assumed to be organized, to escape indeterminacy, and to be subject to the will and understanding of human beings, and, on the other hand, the signs of a new intellectual, moral, religious or metaphysical experience of the world. (Lefort 1988b, 93)

The revolution developed the principals of equality, freedom, human rights, and the notion of popular sovereignty as pivotal references of modern democracy (Lefort 1988a). These principles allow the collective imagination to conceive politics and society in terms of emancipation. Individuals are considered to be citizens and to take part in the political process. Because they are assumed to be mature beings seeking emancipation (Kant 1975) and, because they are equal to each other as Rousseau stated in the social contract, their coming together provides the base for a new social contract and for the formation of the democratic state where the sovereign is the people. From now on, the idea of popular sovereignty works as the matrix of the political and organizes the symbolism and the imaginary of democracy (Lefort 1988a; Diehl 2015).

With this matrix, political representation is figured anew. If in the ancient régime representation was deeply dependent of the king's body, in democracy the power belongs to the people under the precondition that nobody occupies the symbolic place of power. This is the reason why Lefort sustains that the place of power must be kept symbolically empty. In consequence, the configuration of symbolic representation changes from the king's embodiment to what Lefort calls disincorporation. First, there is no person that can be the place of power anymore and, second, society cannot be conceived as an organic body but emerges from dynamic process of networking. The people's representation in democracy is deeply dependent on its symbolic construction, since society is permanently changing, and these changes are integrated in democracy through representation. This dynamic configuration of democratic representation is, on the one hand, an advantage since it allows democracy to better adapt to changes of society. On the other hand, it can be very problematic, as Rosanvallon asserts, generating frustrations and an intrinsic crisis of representation (Rosanvallon 2003).

Temporalities of the Political Imaginary and the Contradictions of Democracy

The political imaginary of democracy is constituted by this dynamic configuration of political representation. It allows individuals to think about society and about themselves in terms of equality and popular sovereignty and it sets free the project of emancipation and autonomy.[2] However, in social and political practice, this normative horizon is not necessarily fully developed. On the contrary, social norms are still coined by hierarchies and discrimination and the relationship between representatives and the people is far from the

---

2   For the elaboration of the concept of political imaginary, cf. Diehl 2015.

idea of delegation of power by the people – here, populist accusa-
tions of misrepresentation by established parties and elites mostly
apply. In the first case, society is still discriminating against some
groups and avoiding the principle of equality defended by the normative horizon of democracy; in the second, popular sovereignty
builds the most important principle of democracy but has still not
been realized in practice, creating the aporia addressed by Rosanvallon (Rosanvallon 2006, 199). Both types of contradictions are
deeply connected with the different temporalities within the democratic imaginary, making the struggle for emancipation, autonomy,
and popular sovereignty a complex and difficult process.

In its first dimension, democracy sets a normative horizon that
allows society to imagine the future in terms of emancipatory space.
This dimension of the political imaginary can be understood as a
normative foundation of democracy and has a long-term temporality, which is engaged with the transformation of the future. The second temporality is connected to social and political norms on the
level of their realization in political and social practices in the actual
time and space. These two dimensions must interact with each other
in order to provide democracy with a stable imagination of the political. The difficulty here is that they do not necessarily evolve in the
same speed, instead they develop two different temporalities de-
pending on historical and cultural situations. This is the reason why
democracy in many cases must deal with contradictions between the
political horizon of emancipation and the current social norms and
practices that do not fully correspond with democratic values. Moreover, there are times when the difference in speed and time between
these two dimensions of the political imaginary increase, creating a
crisis-situation in the full sense of the word. In such situations,
democratic norms are contested and social and political practices
can change very quickly.

Examples of this kind of contradictions are easily detectable in
democracy when the recognition of minorities and the distribution
of civil rights among citizens are in question. In Western democratic
societies, they are well known. Looking at the recent past, examples

such as race segregation in the U.S.A., restrictions of civil and political liberties for women – I have Switzerland in mind, where, in some Cantons, women were allowed to vote only in 1973 – are quite evident. Massimiliano Tomba shows the contradictions within democracy in its very beginning. He pays attention to the exclusion of women, slaves, and the poor in post-revolutionary France in the same time that universalism was stablished as a major principle in the new imagination of society (Tomba 2015).

But the argument of different temporalities between the normative horizon of democracy on the one hand and current social norms or political practices on the other can be equally made concerning the implementation of popular sovereignty. In this case, democracy produces the imagination of the people as the sovereign and concurrently creates procedures limiting the citizens' access to political participation. Such contradictions occurred even if the emancipatory imagination continuously operates, pushing society to become more equal, increase civil and political liberties, and have more popular participation in political decisions. Looking back, one can indeed detect a successful history when it comes to the imagination of equality during the twentieth and beginning of the twenty-first centuries. Minorities are more and more accepted in modern society and their rights have been recognized by law worldwide. This political process, however, has been contested by reactionary and right-wing movements in our days, creating more tensions and, in some cases such as Brazil and the U.S.A., polarizing society. In democratic representation, the struggle for equality and individual emancipation cannot be separated from the struggle for political emancipation and the exercise of popular sovereignty.

Yet, we should not neglect another major source of contradiction: In societies with high levels of inequality, such as in Latin America, or where inequalities are increasing, as we are experiencing in the U.S.A. and Europe as Thomas Piketty (2018) has described, the access of the people to power becomes more and more eclipsed by interest groups, large companies, multinational organizations, and supranational institutions. The exclusion of the poor described by Tomba in post-revolutionary France is still a major problem in modern democracy. After a period of integration of poor classes in the welfare state, the growing inequalities are now bringing back the problem of economic, social, and political exclusion within capitalist societies. According to Oliver Nachtwey, neo-liberal deregulation of the labor market and tax reforms have created a new precarization of large groups of society (Nachtwey 2017, 82). Regressive modernization, as he called it, introduces a depressive perspective on the future generating frustration and increasing the tension within the democratic promise of emancipation and its negation by the representative system, since precarization generates social and political exclusion. For Germany, Armin Schäfer has shown the political effects concerning precarious groups of society reflected in abstention behavior (2015). Colin Crouch (2004) addressed the problem by considering the erosion of democratic institutions. Political institutions such as state institutions and political parties are responsible for the representation of the people and their interests. For Crouch, we are living in a situation where democratic institutions do still exist, but they do not work as they should. Instead, political institutions are eroded in their democratic substance. They are more and more directed by lobbyism, interests of the market, and powerful groups. In such a situation, the democratic task to be performed by political institutions vanishes. The democratic matrix performed by the notion of popular sovereignty cannot generate legitimacy of the government anymore. Citizens become disconnected from the political process in a level that leads democracy to a deep crisis.

From the perspective of the political imaginary, one can say that the two levels of the democratic imaginary do not fully correspond with each other: What becomes visible is the gap between the political normative horizon of emancipation and its realization in social and political practice. Paradoxically, this visibility is a product of the acceptance of the normative horizon of democracy. It is only because the ideals of popular sovereignty, emancipation, and equality are accepted in civil society that citizens can perceive their deficiency in real live.

The Crisis of Representation

In order to understand the crisis of democracy, it is equally important to distinguish two levels of its occurrence. The first is an inherent crisis, which is intrinsic to modern democracy and very much connected to the structure of political representation. The second level of the crisis is connected with particular conjunctures such as economic, social, and political crises. When both levels of crisis come together, they reinforce each other. This is the moment when the crisis challenges democracy deeply. The dynamics of this deep crisis are very complex. For the question of the effects of populism on democratic imagination, I will focus on the role of popular sovereignty in the democratic imaginary and in populism and explore the gap between the normative horizon on the one hand, and social norms and political practices on the other.

On the foundational dimension of the democratic imaginary, popular sovereignty is presupposed as the core element of democracy but, when it comes to the implementation of democratic government, popular sovereignty suffers a transformation: it becomes object of representation. In praxis, the people do not govern, but their representatives do. There is an intrinsic tension within representative democracy: the tension between popular sovereignty and political representation. The balance between both is fragile and depends on the performance of institutions and representatives (Diehl 2019). In consequence, democratic representation is always potentially in crisis. Therefore, the task of political representatives is to moderate the tension between the representation of the people and the principle of popular sovereignty. In addition, if representatives are not able to guarantee the balance between representation and sovereignty of the people, the potential crisis becomes acute (Diehl 2019).

It is possible now to distinguish multiple aspects of a major crisis of democracy we are facing in this very moment.

The first one is the crisis of political communication. Representatives are not able to find the words and the tone to communicate with the citizens they are supposed to represent. This is not only a problem of style but a problem of separation of experiences closely linked to the next aspect of the crisis: the crisis of political institutions, especially the crisis of the political parties. In Europe, since the 1980s, political parties are not able to connect the government and the citizens anymore, and for Latin America and U.S.A., it looks like the same situation is happening now. The next aspect of the crisis is deeper. It is a crisis of representation; citizens do not recognize their demands and their visions in the actions and words of political representatives. In addition, there is a crisis of equality. With increasing economic and social inequalities, the democratic promise of emancipation for all citizens loses the power of shaping the visions for the future. Connecting these four aspects, it becomes clear that citizens become more aware of the gap between the horizon of emancipation and the reality of political practices.

The Blockade of the Political Imaginary

It is because of the crisis of representation that the risk of the blockade of the democratic imaginary becomes immanent. For Pierre Rosanvallon, political imagination can "fall asleep" (Rosanvallon 1988, 137), it can be paralyzed when political representatives and civil society are not able to generate visions for the future. According to Rosanvallon, when political discourse is dominated by the technocratic imagination, the famous TINA "There is no alternative," visions of the future are not possible anymore, that is what he calls "the blockade of the imagination" [blocage de l'imagination] (137). This is a good description of a profound crisis of traditional political parties and representative institutions, when they lose the ability of generating visions for the future and, for this reason, their performative power of shaping the democratic imaginary degrades. In this situation, the confrontation between different political programs is forced back and, instead, an opposition between the masses and elites emerges. Civil society on the one hand and the political system, or rather political institutions, on the other are alienating more and more up to the point where they run into danger that their bond, which is crucial for democracy, could rip apart. These are the key elements of the "populist moment" (Goodwyn 1978).

Populism

Precisely at this point, populism arises and promises to bring the power back to the people and, in so doing, it provides the political imaginary with visions of a future that promise to dissolve all tensions and contradictions in modern democracy. It sets an imagination of an idyllic scenario where people live together without any conflict. Paul Taggart called it the heartland (2000). The heartland is the imaginary home of populism: the dream of harmonious society and the place where the people govern. It sets an imagination of a mythical past that has never happened.

> The heartland is a territory of the imagination. Its explicit invocation occurs only at times of difficulty, and the process yields a notion that is unfocused and yet very powerful as an evocation of that life and those qualities worth defending, thereby stirring populists into political action. The heartland is that place, embodying the aspects of everyday life. (Taggart 2000, 95)

But the populist heartland is different from utopias insofar as it does not build the imagination of an "ideal society," as Taggart observes. Moreover, it casts its "imaginative glances backwards in attempt to construct what has been lost by the present" (95).

I propose to define populism as a political logic that can affect political action, organization, ideology, discourse, and, of course, symbolism. This logic generates a specific narrative that I have called the narrative of the betrayed people (Diehl 2011). This is the story of the people betrayed by the elites and cheated by the established politicians (Tagguieff 2007, 28). In this story, the people constitute a "silent majority" (Taggart 2000, 93) that goes through a process of collective self-awareness, self-organization, and popular mobilization. Following the populist narrative, the people (in the singular) reclaims its own identity and, with the leader's help, can fight for the reconstitution of popular sovereignty (Diehl 2019). This narrative captures the most important features of populism described by scholars in the field: it reinforces popular sovereignty, idealizes the people as virtuous, constructs a strong and Manichean opposition between the people and the elite, is centered on the figure of the leader, and rejects any mediation. The leader builds a direct relationship to the people. This is a very ambivalent political relationship since the leader occupies at the same time a place within the people and above them (Diehl 2019).

In the narrative of the betrayed people, the leader is the vehicle for politicization, since together with the people, the leader builds a block against the elite. According to Ernesto Laclau, the populist logic establishes equivalences between popular demands and transforms particular claims into a single signifier (Laclau 2005). However, that signifier has to be drained out of meaning in order to amalgamate the variety of demands and expectations of the people. For this reason, Laclau calls it "empty signifier" (23). Laclau recognizes the important role of this process in building a political subject: the people that can now claim the power. In this sense, populism operates as an emancipatory factor in the political imaginary. However, the contribution of populism for the democratic imaginary is not the whole story.

Populism and the "End" of Contradictions

Surely, populism can serve as an emancipatory vehicle, but it bears several problems for the democratic imaginary. Populism is a major obfuscator of contradictions and suppressor (in Freudian terms) of tensions within democracy. The first contradiction obfuscated by populism is the one between the normative horizon of popular sovereignty and the weak participation of the people in the exercise of power. This is the Achilles' heel of modern democracy. After the revolutions, democratic politics are legitimized by the principle of popular sovereignty. Yet, in the implementation of democratic government, popular sovereignty is transformed into an object of political representation. On the practical level, the people do not govern, but their representatives do, creating a tension between the idea of popular power and representatives' government. Populism negates precisely this tension. Instead, it draws a picture of a harmonious society as a heartland where the leader and the people are the same, suggesting that the people are now in fact exercising their power.

There is a twist performed by the relationship between the populist leader and the people. In populism, the leader occupies a double position. The leader is regarded as one of the people and, at the same time, as the leader of the people. In the first position, the leader has a horizontal relationship to the people. In the second, she is clearly positioned above the people. As a fellow, the leader must be held accountable to the people, but as a leader, she is the one who guides the people and is able to impose her own decision. In order to resolve this contradiction, populism operates a twist. It presents the leader as identical to the people, so that her actions are considered as the actions of the people. Here, significant similarities to the Hobbesian contract can be detected. As in the Hobbesian model, the individuals transfer their power to the representative – in case of Hobbes to the Leviathan –, but in case of populism, the people are still considered to be the sovereign (Diehl 2019). The populist twist not only obfuscates the contradictions and tensions of democracy, it merges the two temporalities of the political imaginary as well. In populism, the normative horizon of democracy is presented as achieved and the contradictions between this democratic normative horizon on the one hand and the dimension of social norms and political practices on the other seem to be resolved in the close connection between the leader and the people. In some cases, such as Chávez in Venezuela, this close connection culminates in the amalgamation of the leader and the followers, making the necessary distinction between representative and represented impossible.

Populism and the Democratic Imaginary

There is a general risk for democracy produced by populism: The populist twist can, indeed, be the first step to an anti-democratic imagination of power, where the leader *is* the people. In this imagination, popular will and the will of the leader become the same. There is no possibility to control or contest the leader's actions or to sanction her words, since they are supposed to be the same as the people's will. If the twisting movement turns too much, we find ourselves in totalitarianism. This is not only a risk born by right-wing populism but a general risk of populism. The political evolution in Venezuela's case shows how emancipatory demands and emancipatory imagination can be confiscated by the desire to become the leader – Chávez. Sovereignty, which first was imagined as belonging to the people, migrated to the leader. The practical consequences were the damage of the constitutional principle, the weakening of checks and balances, and the loss of liberties.

In many cases such as Austria, Hungary, Poland, and Brazil, the twist caused by populism is aggravated by the combination with right-wing extremist ideologies. Right-wing populism is far more problematic than other populist varieties. Since right-wing populism conceives the people as a homogeneous body, which value is to be pure (culturally, ethnically, racially, religiously, etc.), it negates the principle of equality and, sometimes even advocates for the restriction of freedom – some Pegida[3] followers, for example, demand less liberty. Generally, the visions of right-wing populism are reactionary, emphasizing the loss of an imaginary past.

To put it in a nutshell, populism is not totalitarian or authoritarian and can indeed reinforce democracy by setting free the imagination of the people as the political subject. It can be an important tool for politicization and political mobilization, since it puts forward the imagination of a collective political actor searching for emancipa-

---

3   Pegida is a German protest movement that stands in the tradition of German nationalism and advocates xenophobic, anti-Islam, and far-right politics.

tion and asks for more popular sovereignty. The flipside, however, is the possibility of populism to become the first step towards totalitarianism. For this reason, the relationship between populism in general and democracy is ambivalent.

Nevertheless, when populism is combined with right-wing extremist ideologies and builds right-wing populism, it defines the people as a body to be protected from heterogeneous elements. In this case, at least one of the pillars of the democratic imaginary is damaged: the idea of equality. Right-wing populism does not recognize equality among members of society. Instead, it defines the people by constructing a homogeneous core, a pure ethnical, cultural, and even racial image of society. It can take a fascist shape such as in Bolsonaro's case in Brazil or a postmodernist form like Donald Trump in the U.S.A. or Pim Fortyun in the Netherlands, but it is deeply connected to the fear of contamination of the people's body. Here, one of the pillars of democratic visions of the future, equality, is broken. And, indeed, the contradiction between the normative horizon of equality and the unequal social norms or political practices disappears since there is no expectation of universal equality anymore. In this sense, right-wing populism operates as a reactionary matrix, trying to reverse the normative horizon set by the democratic imaginary.

In countries where right-wing populism is in power, such as Hungary, Turkey, and Brazil, both threats for democracy can simultaneously occur. The totalitarian and authoritarian potentiality of the populist twist is combined with the exclusivist imagination of the people's body, reinforcing racism, xenophobia, antisemitism, anti-Muslim, anti-feminism, anti-gender politics, etc. In this case, the imaginary is not blocked, as in the case of crisis of democracy, but it is not the democratic imaginary anymore.

Works Cited

Castoriadis, Cornelius. 1987. *The Imaginary Institution of Society.* Cambridge, MA: MIT Press.

Crouch, Colin. 2004. *Post-Democracy.* Cambridge: Polity Press.

Diehl, Paula. 2011. "Die Komplexität des Populismus – Ein Plädoyer für ein mehrdimensionales und graduelles Konzept." *Totalitarismus und Demokratie* 8.2: 273-291.

———. 2015. *Das Symbolische, das Imaginäre und die Demokratie. Eine Theorie politischer Repräsentation.* Baden-Baden: Nomos Verlag.

———. 2019. "The Populist Twist. The Relationship Between the Leader and the People in Populism." *Creating Political Presence. Theorizing the New Politics of Representation*, ed. Johannes Pollak and Dario Castiglione, 110-137. Chicago: University of Chicago Press.

Goodwyn, Lawrence. 1978. *The Populist Moment. A Short History of Agrarian Revolt in America.* New York: Oxford University Press.

Laclau, Ernesto. 2005. *On Populist Reason.* London: Verso.

Lefort, Claude. 1988a. "The Question of Democracy." *Democracy and Political Theory*, 9-20. Dales Brewery/Oxford: Polity Press.

———. 1988b. "Interpreting Revolution within the French Revolution." *Democracy and Political Theory*, 89-114. Dales Brewery/Oxford: Polity Press.

Kant, Immanuel. 1975. "Beantwortung auf die Frage: Was ist Aufklärung?" *Kant: Was ist Aufklärung? Aufsätze zur Geschichte und Philosophie*, ed. Jürgen Zehbe, 55-61. Göttingen: Vandenhoeck & Ruprecht. Orig. pub. 1784.

Nachtwey, Oliver. 2017. *Die Abstiegsgesellschaft: Über das Aufbegehren in der regressiven Moderne.* Frankfurt am Main: Edition Suhrkamp.

Piketty, Thomas. 2018. *Top Incomes in France in the Twentieth Century: Inequality and Redistribution, 1901-1998.* Cambridge, MA: Harvard University Press.

Rosanvallon, Pierre. 1988. "Malaise dans la représentation." *La République du centre. La fin de l'exception française,* ed. François Furet, Jacques Juillard, and Pierre Rosanvallon, 132-182. Paris: Calmann-Lévy.

———. 2003. *Pour une histoire conceptuelle du politique.* Paris: Seuil.

———. 2006. *Democracy Past and Future,* ed. Samuel Moyn. New York: Columbia University Press.

Schäfer, Armin. 2015. *Der Verlust politischer Gleichheit. Warum die sinkende Wahlbeteiligung der Demokratie schadet.* Schriften aus dem Max-Planck-Institut für Gesellschaftsforschung, Vol. 81. Frankfurt: Campus.

Taggart, Paul. 2000. *Populism.* Buckingham/Philadelphia: Open University Press.

Tagguieff, Pierre-André. 2007. *L'illusion populiste. Essai sur les démagogies de l'âge démocratique.* Paris: Flammarion.

Tomba, Massimilano. 2015. "1793: The Neglected Legacy of Insurgent Universality." *History of the Present: A Journal of Critical History* 5.2: 109-136.

In the Shadow of Tomorrow:
Biological Entanglements, Genetic Editing, and a New Techno-Utopia in the Americas

RÜDIGER KUNOW

Abstract

In this paper, I seek to explore how advances in micro-biology and the biotech sector are fundamentally changing how people think of their lives and the lives of others. While genetics is producing new utopias of the human life course, promising new opportunities for combatting serious diseases and improving everybody's daily lives, it is at the same time also undergoing a process of radical democratization. Biohacking, or DIY biology, is a fast-growing movement involving people from all walks of life and on all skill levels. They come together in improvised laboratories, even garages, to experiment on the building blocks of human life. Although biohacking so far is a predominantly U.S.-American affair, it is fast expanding all over the Americas and, in doing so, invites renewed reflections about the unequal production and distribution of knowledge in a key area for the future well-being of humans.

Hacking Life, the Democratization of Science and a New Culture of Life

When school is over for Elodie Rebesque, a 16 year-old high school senior from California, what is on her mind is not chilling with friends; she has more serious, even ambitious plans. She sets out for *Biocurious*, an open-science community lab only a few blocks away and here she spends most of her spare time on what might be called advanced bio-tech research. She is very serious about this. Through her work in the laboratory, she hopes to discover nothing less than a new, genetically based cure for her brother's bouts of spontaneous pneumothorax, a critical disease which causes air to accumulate in the pleural space making it impossible for patients to breathe. Ultimately, spontaneous pneumothorax can result in a life-threatening collapse of the lungs. Assisted by mentors, Elodie works on a genetic modification, changing the working of proteins which bind her brother's outer lungs to his pleural cavity (Pauwells 2018), thus bettering his condition.

The scene here is Los Altos, CA, but it could just as well be São Paulo or Mexico City. Thousands of similar labs like Biocurious with names like Genspace, SyntechBio, or Biohackademy and Hackeando la vida, have opened up all over the Americas, as non-profit organizations are promoting easy and often low-priced access to the arcana of synthetic biology, biotechnology, and especially genetics. In such venues, some of them linked to universities, others to non-profit organizations, and often outside the purview of the science establishment, sensitive scientific knowledge and procedures are becoming available to non-professionals in the spirit of what some call "open science." And not everybody involved here is motivated by Elodie's philanthropic goals, as in the much-publicized example of someone producing luminescent plants (Griffiths 2014). Even though, as this example shows, not all that is going on in this field is exclusively focused on humans, the great allure of the ongoing research and experimentation is that the building blocks of life have become open to investigation, but also to intervention and perhaps even manipulation.

I am using "biohacking" as an umbrella term to describe activities like Elodie's if for no other reason than that is has become the most current term among the genetic engineering lay, do-it-yourself community. It also conveys a sense of transgression, of going beyond customary standards which is certainly reflected in much of the rhetoric of those involved (Meyer 2014). Biohackers, wherever they work, are certainly a motley crowd and one should be careful not to rush to generalizations. What seems to be reasonably clear, though, is that the movement is both highly diverse and international in its outreach. DIYbio.org, founded in 2008, "with the mission of establishing a vibrant, productive and safe community of DIY biologists," offers an impressive list of ongoing activities, community labs, start-ups, local groups, etc. Its most recent project is DIYbiosphere, "an open-source project to connect DIY bio-related activities worldwide" (DIYbio.org).

Even so, biohacking so far is a predominantly U.S.-American affair which will for this reason also be the principal focus of this paper. This is not to say, however, that it is not also quickly expanding all over the Americas, often under less favorable conditions than in Elodie's case. As I hope to show in the following pages, biohacking has developed into a major hub of Inter-American connections and entanglements, not all of them effective and enabling. As a group of biohackers from different locations in Latin America notes, "The groups from the U.S. can buy used equipment online and get donations of old equipment from universities and research centers. Their Latin American counterparts don't have these possibilities, and must instead build low-cost versions of standard equipment" (Ochoa et al. 2016). What has been hailed by some as the Rise of Citizen Bioscience is already now producing new asymmetries and reinforcing old ones. This situation invites renewed reflections about technology transfer between the Americas and beyond about equality of access to the most advanced scientific technologies of our time, technologies which are crucially important for the future well-being of humans. Such a reflection, however, will have to be the topic of another paper, since this essay is concerned not with offering a comparative survey of biohacking activities in the Americas,[1] but rather with charting the cultural and ethical entanglements produced by the democratization of genetic knowledge and technologies.

---

1   Such surveys, some of them written in a celebratory mood, can be found in Mukherjee and specifically for the South American scene in Cruz et al. 2016 or Wade et al. 2015.

Biohacking, in its institutional but certainly even more so in its DIY forms, is of course a multi-faceted process involving a wide range of procedures and motivations (Meyer 2013; Mukherjee 2017, 306-315). In the following, and working from a cultural-critical perspective, I will be reading biohacking as essentially a *utopian gesture*, energized by what Ernst Bloch (1995, 75) called "anticipatory consciousness," a consciousness of "the Not-yet, of what has objectively not yet been there." In biohacking, this "anticipatory consciousness" has found a new, possibly its ultimate object, the human body, and also a new direction: it is no longer concerned with awaiting the future, but instead aims to control it. This means that a new utopia is taking shape in the field of biology and speaking in its idiom. And because the object of this utopian project is nothing less than the future of human life, it is perhaps the most emotionally charged utopia in human history. The biohacking utopia is not about the far-away Neverland of former times. It is about here and now and brought into being by state-of-the-art technology. Taking the future of life into your own hands has been hailed by some as democratization of the most advanced regions of scientific knowledge (DIYbio.org). While professional genetics is rapidly expanding its capabilities and outreach, its popular DIY sister is attracting more and more lay practitioners, so that genetics in all its forms is becoming "one of the key sites for the fabrication of the contemporary self" (Novas and Rose 2000, 490)

What especially warrants critical attention are a number of important shifts of perspective and emphasis which come with the brave new world of genetics. When the ultimate DIY object becomes human life, this marks a changeover from the public and political (planning a new society) to the private; from the collective (the body politic) to the single, individual body; and here from the visible to the invisible, intimate recesses of human embodiment.

This new kind of utopia is emerging at a historical moment when other, older utopian energies seem to have become exhausted, when it has become virtually impossible to imagine a world beyond and outside the current capitalist dispensation. However, as my argument will show, this new utopia is a techno-utopia which is crucially dependent on, and hence deeply entangled in current formations of neoliberal capitalism.

"Wonders of the Invisible World": The Cultural Promises of Genetics and Biohacking

What the atom was during the Cold War period, the gene is quickly becoming today. The most forceful and disquieting concept metaphor which travels intensely and insistently from science to society and is captivating both experts and the general public alike. Its hour of power came on June 26, 2000, when a group of scientists accompanied by President Bill Clinton took the stage and proudly announced that the mapping of the genes of the human genome had finally been completed (Hood and Rowan 2013; Craig Venter 2007). The dawning "golden age of biotechnology," as Leon R. Kass, former Chair of the President's Council on Bioethics, called it (Kass 2003, 9), is marked by a paradigm shift in biology, a shift from explanation to manipulation (Mukherjee 2017, 11), from biology as destiny to biology as design. This is without doubt the most utopian-minded field of knowledge production in our time. It is filled with seemingly unlimited promises for improving, even refashioning the biology of human life.

For the purposes of the present paper and its cultural-critical argument I propose is to read genes and genetic diagnosis as an *archeology of the future*.[2] Hidden deep inside a body, and brought to light by state-of-the-art high tech procedures, an individual's genetic endowment nests the future of their life. At the same time, this new knowledge about the future invites measures in the here and now – biohacking – to protect this person from real or assumed dangers that loom in the time to come.

---

2   I am echoing here the title of a book by Jameson, *Archeologies of the Future: The Desire Called Utopia and Other Science Fictions* (2005).

As a future-directed operation, biohacking actually dissolves the stability of the Enlightenment body; it opens up its hidden recesses, promises to reveal its buried secrets, and then to rearrange its future course in accordance with human dreams and desires (Kunow 2018, 325-369). Among the "wonders of the invisible world," which geneticists and their advocates in the general public almost routinely point to, are the prospects of controlling the previously unforeseen contingencies of life. Especially the "availability of predictive genetic testing introduces a qualitative [sic] new dimension … it is becoming possible for individuals to be identified as genetically at risk for a particular condition prior to any symptoms appearing" (Rose 2007, 107). Showcase examples of these predictive capabilities are genetically based diseases like Chorea Huntington, a progressive breakdown of nerve cells in the brain. If one parent has the Chorea gene, the chances for a child to inherit the parent's deadly disease are up to 50%. Genetic research has also identified the genetic basis of a number of other genetic pathologies, such as cystic fibrosis (called Mukoviszidose in Germany), Down Syndrome (or trisomia 21), and BRCA-1 and 2. The latter's link to breast cancer has become publicly known in the wake of actress Angelina Jolie's decision to undergo double mastectomy. Genetic causes of other malfunctions, this time of brain functions such as autism or bipolar disorder, but also a broad range of other undesirables not directly tied to the body, such as bodily aging or criminal behavior, are also being discussed in the scientific community and even more so in the general public. Thus, the echo of Cotton Mather's work by that title (1693) is here both intentional and ironic. Mather's obsession with the secret machinations of the devil is in our day echoed in a similar obsession, especially in debates about the equally underground, surreptitious workings of genes to produce socially undesired consequences (Mukherjee 2017, 459-461).

Such genetically based ideas circulate widely, less so perhaps in the scientific community of specialists than in the general public. In fact, "much of what people know about biomedical science comes from the press and from the experts in the self-help market" (Pitts-

Taylor 1997, 641). It is this popularization of new scientific knowledges which makes them a matter of concern also for us in Cultural Critique. If genetics is a new biological utopia, then it certainly has its complications. While there is a real chance for decreasing the incidence of serious genetically based illnesses and human suffering, genetic interventions, professional or amateur ones produce new urgencies. One is that the call for intervention may in the future become compulsive. And if being identified as "genetically at risk" through serious genetic anomalies such as Chorea Huntington, muscular dystrophy and others is or certainly feels like a suspended death sentence, then the identification of ethnic or social groups as genetically risky constitutes a new form of marginalization (Fletcher 2008).

Under the programmatic title "The Future Is Now," Beth Fletcher et al. describe the "issues involved in developing carrier screening programs in the United States" (2008, 33). Interestingly, the issues involved here read like a course program in multiculturalism. The authors (most of them medical geneticists) report how different ethno-cultural and religious groups across the country react to genetic screening programs, with special emphasis on Ashkenazi Jews, African Americans, and Latino/as. The edited collection *Racial Identities, Genetic Ancestry, and Health in South America: Argentina, Brazil, Colombia, and Uruguay* presents material showing how genetics interacts with the multicultural composition of nation states in South America (Penchaszadeh 2011, 219-229). In this perspective, genetics is not a "neutral" field of scientific knowledge production; rather, "cultural issues need to be taken into account," and it is these issues that guide or misguide people to be tested (Fletcher et al. 2008, 35) and the possibility of their targeted as carriers of potential genetic risks.

Since 2012, genetics have moved on to the new levels of feasibility. CRISPR-cas9 is a technology which makes it possible to make specific, targeted alterations already in living cells, not only to delete undesirable genetic information but also to *add* new information (in)to the human genome. CRISPR has spread rapidly through the sciences as well as into general culture. It is fast, efficient, affordable, and considerably easier to use, making biohacking procedures like Elodie Rebesque's eminently feasible. Reproduction has so far been the principal context in which such procedures have been performed and also intensely and contentiously discussed. After all, genetic editing raises troubling ethical questions, as even a Harvard-based stem cell researcher George Daley admits: "Genetic editing raises the most fundamental of issues about how we are going to view our humanity in the future and whether we are going to take the dramatic step of modifying our own germ line and in a sense take control of our genetic destiny ..." (Daley, quoted in Mukherjee 2017, 476).

In the future, even the very near future, genetic editing in various contexts will very probably become a routine procedure. In a recent piece for the *Village Voice*, Zoë Schlanger reports on New York City's first do-it-yourself genetic laboratory: "They'd all come to learn how to use CRISPR, molecular 'tools' derived from the chemistry of microbes that have taken the bioengineering world from messing with yeast DNA to editing human embryos in four years flat" (Schlanger 2016). The irony that is noticeable in this report loses some of its acumen when one is looking at most recent developments. When I was working on this paper, and while a number of signals were pointing into this direction (Mukherjee 2017, 477), I did not anticipate that scientific "progress" would catch up so quickly with reflections such as the one presented here. In November of 2018, scientists from the Southern University of Science in China announced that they had released into the world the first two gene-edited twin babies (Lagomarsino 2019). CRISPR-cas9-based genetic engineering has been performed on them with the ostensible purpose of immunizing them against their father's HI-deficiency. I do not wish to rehearse here the controversial debate about this breakthrough or perhaps rather breach; instead I want to use this stunning event to emphasize the moral and cultural entanglements produced by genetic editing and the choices underwriting such operations, choices which are personal but at the same time also cultural and political. In this latter context, we should not forget that the genetic research at Southern University is part of a massive effort by the Chinese government to become world leader in genetics (100,000 Genome Project). Rumors even have it that efforts are underway to sequence the so-called "Han" gene – if it actually exists – thus offering a biological proof for national Chinese identity. In this context, it seems worthwhile pointing also to the Mexican Genome Diversity Project (MGDP) which attempted to harness genomic research to the idea of Mexican uniqueness or "Mexicanhood." Specifically, it was against the background of experiences of dispossession in "archaeology, botany or zoology ... that the novelty of population genomics became amenable to be understood as a sovereign matter" (Schwartz Marín 2011, 2).

In many locations across the Americas, genetic editing has moved from the laboratory to general culture, speaking the idiom of state-of-the-art science with a decidedly political inflection. As Wade et al. report in their overview of genetic research in South and Central America, research on genetic ancestry and genetic admixture – usually phrased in terms of European, African and Amerindian ancestries – might shape people's ideas about the nation and its diversity, especially in relation to 'race' (including heredity and appearance), both at a collective and individual level, especially in South American nations" (Wade et al. 2015, 776).

Whatever the political ambitions involved, taking part in the CRISPR adventure and exploring its utopian potential still remains a question of access, funding, and finding a cultural imaginary in which it can make "sense." As Peter Mills, assistant director of the Nuffield Council on Bioethics argues, with regard to conditions in many South American nations, one can imagine a 'liberation genomics' that self-consciously harnesses the extraordinary potential of genome editing in the interests of social, global and intergenerational justice. Securing the social benefits of genome editing, requires us to ask how the public interest is constituted and articulated in the public sphere at different levels, and how, attending to the determinants of social, political and moral geography, a project of relating local and global public interests can be defined (Mills 2016). "Liberation genomics" with its political echoes (liberation theology) is certainly a tantalizing proposition. However, its realization does not only depend on the elusive dynamics of scientific "progress," but also on the political, social, and especially economic conditions which form its inevitable context.[3] So, we need to take with the proverbial grain of salt such grandiloquent statements as this: "nature may, after all, be entirely approachable," coming from geneticist Thomas Morgen (quoted in Mukherjee 2017, 11).

Life Constantly in Advance of Itself: Genomic and Eugenics

Biohacking, or what scientists call directed or "defined genetic change" (Mukherjee 2017, 489), does not in itself have any clear definition or a singular widely shared purpose. This is even more so when we look at its repercussions in the general culture. What does seem reasonably clear though at this point is that more and more people across the Americas, especially young ones such as Elodie, are growing up with the expectation that taking control through genetic change of their body's make-up, and thus their future, is both possible and desirable. Already now more and more people are checking their own genetic make-up and are even more concerned about their partner having "bad genes." The term is usually understood as referring to a wide array of defective mental and physical conditions, beyond the usual suspects just mentioned. The specter of "bad genes" is giving rise to a range of further practices – many of DIY character – as drawing up "pedigree charts" previously been used in animal breeding (Kevles 1985; Stillwell 2012). These are being recommended by "experts" as offering "scientific" information on the likelihood of a genetic disorder running in a particular

---

3   Hilary Cunningham has explored how genetics functions inside "the globalization of the economy (particularly in the areas of intellectual property rights and biotechnology patents)" and impacts especially on the rights and options of indigenous peoples (Cunningham 1989).

family and thus to assist in finding a partner with desirable traits. There is little doubt that in contexts such as these, DIY genetics or biohacking are having far-reaching consequences for how people live their lives, whom they choose as partners, and what expectations they have concerning their life course. This promotes an ablest imaginary of human body and human life whose ultimate goal is that of having a body "better than well,"[4] a body that can hold out against the vicissitudes of human life in time.

This meliorist and ablist[5] agenda of biohacking brings to light affinities, undesirable ones, which tend to be forgotten in the celebratory can-do mood of many DIY discourses: its link with eugenics. There is more than a semantic similarity between gen-etics and eu-gen-ics involved here: both are essentially responses to anxieties, cultural, not biological responses to anxieties about the future of the body, the individual body as well as the body politic. During its heyday in the first half of the twentieth century, eugenics was quite outspoken about the need to intervene in people's biological endowment with the purpose of avoiding physical and moral degeneration. In this spirit, Ernest A. Hooton, at a meeting of the American Association for the Advancement of Science called for a "biological new deal which will segregate and sterilize the anti-social mentally unfit" (quoted in Himes 1935, 21). This was 1935 and was until recently probably best reckoned among the abominations of the past. But with the advent of genetics, some of the old specters reappeared. Gerald Leach's clarion call for "breeding better people" (quoted in Mukherjee 2017, 272) goes back to the 1970s, but it could just as well have come from some DIY biohacking activist of our own day (for this rhetoric see e.g., the posts of Mike Flanagan@ ChesterOrNot). Robert L. Sinsheimer, an internationally acclaimed

---

4 This argument is more fully unfolded in Carl Elliot's book by that title.

5 Ableism is here understood as "a network of beliefs, processes and practices that produces a particular kind of self and body (the corporeal standard) that is projected as the perfect, species-typical, and therefore essential and fully human" (Campbell 2009, 5).

geneticist and a pioneer in creating functional strands of DNA in the laboratory, makes the underlying continuities between past and present explicit, unapologetically so: "The old eugenics was limited to the numerical enhancement of the best of our existing gene pool. The new eugenics would in principle allow the *conversion* of the unfit to the highest genetic level" (quoted in Kay 1993, 276; emphasis original). Sinsheimer was a highly-placed insider at the interface of science and politics, was also involved in research and grant-giving activities across the Americas, via the Rockefeller Foundation. Given his position, such a statement does carry some weight. However, his argument does not simply invoke once again visions of a new biological utopia of human perfection of everybody, from a cultural-critical perspective it is his choice of words which warrants a closer look. I am reading it as an update of the eugenics rhetoric of the past, advocating, perhaps even celebrating the survival of genetically fittest.

What is more, genetic change, or what I am here calling bio-hacking, comes in the perspective opened by Sinsheimer to be endowed with a quasi-religious aura: it is seen as essentially a conversion experience.[6] This does not simply rehearse previous associations of science with religion, the scientist as demiurge. More importantly, it projects a vision of human life in the future which has a very distinct U.S.-American genealogy, one that is deeply rooted in the nation's cultural heritage. What I am suggesting here is that genetics and especially its DIY variant, biohacking, may well be understood as the re-emergence of an old acquaintance in new, admittedly hi-tech, garb: the Puritan ethic. I think the case can be made that there is quite a dose of Puritan thinking in genetic testing and

---

6   It may be interesting to note that Sinsheimer's rhetoric with its religious echoes ties in with an overall tendency in the genomics research community to invest its work with a transcendental aura. When the Human Genome Project was officially declared completed, Leon R. Kass, former Chairman of the President's Council on Bioethics described the effort as rewriting "The Book of Life," a kind of biological bible. Interestingly, he published his findings under the title "New Atlantis."

intervention, in the biohacking activism of our day, energized as it is by the insistent demand to constantly better yourself. After all, the Puritans believed in "the outward and visible sign of inward election," as *The Book of Common Prayer* put it. Their latter-day successors in the DIY biohacking scene similarly believe in a necessary link between outside and inside of the body, only that this time the outward signs of inner (this time biological) depravity, based on anomalies in the genomic endowment of human beings, can be corrected, not by becoming a better person but a better-constructed person, and biohacking is the way. One might characterize this as the reconstitution of the formerly Puritan self in the guise of the *genetically Elect*. It also marks a conceptual and moral move from *doing good* to *being good*.

I would like to contrast briefly this U.S.-American genealogy with a different one that is particularly salient in the South and Central American context. Populations here have long been subject to genetic analysis, and not always with benevolent intentions. Bio hacking is necessarily situated in this historical context, even as this lineage is as yet largely unexplored. As observers like Wade et al. note, "Latin America is a little-explored region for addressing these questions [that follow in the wake of genetic interventions]: the existing literature focuses mainly on the United States and Europe" (778). Nonetheless there are some indications that *hackeando la vida* in South and Central America solicits cultural resonances that differ markedly from those in other parts of the world. On the basis of findings from a project about genetic testing in Brazil, Columbia, and Mexico, researchers noted the ambivalent impact of genetics on notions of nation and "race." They were particularly concerned about possible renewed entanglements of science with biologistic arguments (Penchaszadeh 2011).[7] The same context plays a role also in the Mexican genome project mentioned above. Some of the public resonances of this project were focusing on issues of genomic nationalism or bio-based sovereignty (Schwartz Marín 2011, 156-160).

---

7   Cf. the discussion in González Burchard et al. 2003.

The material presented here offers mere glimpses at a highly complex set of entanglements produced across the Americas by "pure science" in its most advanced and powerful form. These glimpses nevertheless are a timely reminder that whatever the intentions involved in each case, biohacking does not exist apart from its social and cultural contexts, contexts which are determined by capitalism in its latest, neoliberal formation. And here, we need to keep in mind that, especially in the South American context, "one of the most salient features of the discourse on [CRISPR] ... has been the battle over the intellectual property rights to the underlying technology" (Mills 2016).[8] I have elsewhere shown how much neoliberal capitalism is interested in, even interlaced with, biotech and especially genetic research and the profits to be derived from it (Kunow 2018, 365-367). Given a popular culture that, not only in the U.S. but also in South America (Chile and Brazil are examples here), increasingly valorizes self-surveillance and self-quantification in coercive fitness regimes ("track your stats"), biohacking is not the disinterested quest for knowledge even as this kind of knowledge gets increasingly valorized. Already now, insurance companies are offering "incentives" to people who give access to their genetic information, arguing that there is really no difference between generic information and other health-related information (Rose 2007, 122). Under the conditions of neoliberalism and its relentless battle in North, but also South/Central America alike, against health care and social security, biohacking may soon become a well-considered act of self-defense, of bracing yourself for a life without a social safety net.

Conclusion: "Making Ourselves a Little Better"?

Biohacking, DIY genetic interventions of various kinds are the cornerstones of a new and powerful *biological utopia*, a techno-utopia

---

8   A private company, Utah-based "Myriad Genetics" has been granted a patent for the BRCA-1 genetic sequence, the first ever granted for a human gene sequence (Mukherjee 2017, 439).

based on the most advanced knowledges of our time. They seem to provide feasible shortcuts towards a perfect future life for individuals and whole collectivities and in doing so give rise to a new health populism for whom a person's corporeal endowments are the object of constant attention, apprehension, and intervention. While presumably enhancing the performance of the human body and thus the quality of life, it provides, the newly available procedures have also increased the overall sense of uncertainty about what may come: "[T]he sense that some, perhaps all, persons, though existentially healthy are actually asymptomatically or pre-symptomatically ill" (Rose 2007, 19) adds new urgencies, produces new apprehensions to which biohacking may provide at least a temporary reprieve. In this context, a whole new "regime of living" (Collier and Lakoff 2015, 22, 39) is emerging in many places across the Americas, one which turns the injunction of the Delphi Oracle in ancient Greece (γνῶθι σεαυτόν [know yourself]) into an imperative of self-preservation: know your genes so that you can control your future.

Works Cited

Berger, Ronald J. 2013. *Introducing Disability Studies*. London: Boulder.

Bloch, Ernst. 1995. *The Principle of Hope*. Cambridge: MIT Press.

Campbell, Fiona Kumari. 2009. *Contours of Ableism. The Production of Disability and Abledness*. Houndmills, Basigstoke: Palgrave Macmillan.

Collier, Stephen J., and Andrew Lakoff. 2015. "Vital Systems Security: Reflexive Biopolitics and the Government of Emergency." *Theory, Culture and Society* 32.2: 19-51.

Craig Venter, John. 2007. *A Life Decoded: My Genome, My Life*. New York: Viking.

Cruz, Edgar, Andrés Ochoa, Oscar Joel de la Barrera, Benavidez Manuel Giménez, Maria Chavez, and Marie-Anne Van Sluys.

2016. "The biohacking landscape in Latin America". https://www._oreilly.com/ideas/biohacking-latin-america/.

Cunningham, Hilary. 1989. "Colonial Encounters in Postcolonial Contexts: Patenting Indigenous DNA and the Human Genome Diversity Project." *Critique of Anthropology* 18.2: 205-233.

Elliott, Carl. 2003. *Better Than Well: American Medicine Meets the American Dream*. New York: Norton.

Fletcher, Beth A., Susan J. Gross, Kristin G. Monoghan, Deborah A. Driscoll, and Michael S. Watson. 2008. "The Future Is Now: Carrier Screening for All Populations." *Genetics in Medicine* 10: 33-36.

González Burchard, Esteban et al. 2003. "The importance of race and ethnic background in biomedical research and clinical practice." *New England Journal of Medicine* 348.12: 1170-1175.

Griffiths, Andy. 2014. "World's first glow-in-the-dark plant genetically engineered." *Dezeen, January* 13, 2014. https://www.dezeen.com/2014/01/13/worlds-first-glow-in-the-dark-plant-genetically-engineered/.

Himes, Norman E. 1935. "News from the U.S.A." *The Eugenics Review* 27.1: 21-24.

Hood, Leroy, and Lee Rowan. 2013. "The Human Genome Project: Big Science Transforms Biology and Medicine." *Genome Medicine* 5.9: 79.

Jameson, Fredric. 2005. *Archeologies of the Future: The Desire Called Utopia and Other Science Fictions*. London: Verso.

Kass, Leon R. 2003. "Ageless Bodies, Happy Souls: Biotechnology and the Pursuit of Perfection." *The New Atlantis* 1: 9-28.

Kay, Lily E. 1993. *The Molecular Vision of Life: Caltech, the Rockefeller Foundation, and the Rise of the New Biology*. New York: Oxford University Press.

Kevles, Daniel J. 1985. *In the Name of Eugenics: Genetics and the Uses of Human Heredity*. New York: Knopf.

Kunow, Rüdiger. 2018. *Material Bodies: Biology and Culture in the United States*. Heidelberg: Winter

Lagomarsino, Valentina. 2019. "Arrival of Gene-edited Babies. What Lies Ahead?" Harvard University Blog, March 19. http://sitn.hms.harvard.edu/flash/2019/arrival-gene-edited-babies-lies-ahead/.

Meyer, Morgan. 2014. "Hacking Life? The Politics and Poetics of DIY Biology. Paper at the Workshop on the Research Agendas in the Societal Aspects of Synthetic Biology". https://cns.asu.edu/sites/default/files/meyerm_synbiopaper2edit_2014.pdf.

————. 2013. "Domesticating and democratizing science: a geography of do-it-yourself biology." *Journal of Material Culture* 18.2: 117-134.

Mills, Peter. 2016. "CRISPR in South America: A Case for 'Liberation Genomics'?" *Nuffield Council on Bioetheics*, November 9. http://nuffieldbioethics.org/blog/crispr-south-america-case-liberation-genomics. Blog.

Mukherjee, Siddhartha. 2017. *The Gene: An Intimate History*. New York: Vintage.

Novas, Carlos, and Nikolas Rose. 2000. "Genetic Risk and the Birth of the Somatic Individual." *Economy and Society* 28: 485-513.

Pauwells, Eleonore. 2018. "The Rise of Citizen Bioscience." *Scientific American*, January 5. https://blogs.scientificamerican.com/observations/the-rise-of-citizen-bioscience/.

Penchaszadeh, Victor B. 2011. "Forced Disappearance and Suppression of Identity of Children in Argentina. Experiences in Genetic Identification." *Racial Identities, Genetic Ancestry, and Health in South America: Argentina, Brazil, Colombia, and Uruguay*, ed. Sarah Gibbon, Ricardo Ventura Santos, and Mónika Sans, 213-242. New York: Palgrave.

Pitts-Taylor, Victoria. 1997. "The Plastic Brain: Neoliberalism and the Neuronic Self." *Health* 14.6: 635-652.

Ochoa, Edgar Andrés, Oscar Joel de la Barrera, Benavidez Manuel Giménez, Maria Chavez, and Marie-Anne Van Sluys. 2016. "The biohacking landscape in Latin America: A look at the biohacking spaces in Latin America and the open-science initiatives that are expanding in the region." *Oreilly.com*, May 2. https://www.oreilly.com/ideas/biohacking-latin-america/.

Rose, Nicholas. 2007. *The Politics of Life Itself: Biomedicine, Power, and Subjectivity in the Twenty-First Century*. Princeton: Princeton University Press.

Schlanger, Zoë. 2016. "In Brooklyn, Even Genetic Engineering Has Gone DIY." *The Village Voice*, June 22.

Schwartz Marín, Ernesto. 2011. *Genomic Sovereignty and the 'Mexican Genome': An Ethnography of Postcolonial Biopolitics*. Phil. Diss. University of Exeter.

Stillwell, Devon. 2012. "Eugenics visualized: The Exhibit of the Third International Congress of Eugenics, 1932." *Bulletin of the History of Medicine* 86.2: 206-236.

Synbiomx.org. 2017. "Biohacking en México: talento y visión." August 7. https://synbiomx.org/2017/07/08/biohacking-en-mexico-Talento-y-vision.

Wade, Peter, Carlos López-Beltrán, Eduardo Restrepo, and Ricardo Ventura Santos. 2015. "Genomic Research, Publics and Experts in Latin America: Nation, Race and Body." *Social Studies of Science* 45.6: 775-796.

Contributors

Carolina Crespo obtained her PhD in social anthropology from the University of Buenos Aires. She is an investigator at the National Council of Scientific and Technical Research and professor at the University of Buenos Aires. She works on cultural and ethnic heritage and archive and memory politics in Patagonia, Argentina. She examines, under an ethnographic approach, processes of memories and silences construction with *mapuches* within the framework of ethno-territorial claims and political struggles. Crespo has published several articles about subaltern memories, indigenous subjectivities, ethno-territorial claims, archaeological heritage, and museums exhibitions. She received an award for her published undergraduate research: *Cruces y tensiones sociales (en)mascaradas. Las fiestas de carnaval de Gualeguaychú* (Colección Folklore y Antropología Nº 5. Secretaría de Cultura de la provincia de Santa Fe) She edited the volume *Tramas de la diversidad. Patrimonio y Pueblos Originarios* (Antropofagia, 2013), and compiled other books with other anthropologists including Flora Losada and Alicia Martín, *Patrimonio, Políticas Culturales y Participación Ciudadana* (Antropofagia, 2007); Hernán Morel and Margarita Ondelj, *La política cultural en debate. Diversidad, performance y patrimonio cultural* (CICCUS, 2015); and Ana Ramos and María Alma Tozzini, *Memorias en lucha. Recuerdos y silencios en contextos de subordinación y alteridad* (Colección Aperturas, UNRN, forthcoming).

Paula Diehl is a Professor of Political Theory and History of Ideas at the Christian-Albrechts-University Kiel. She holds a PhD from the Humboldt University Berlin and has a degree in sociology and communication studies. Paula Diehl was the principal investigator of the projects "Conceptualizing the political imagination," "Symbolism of democracy," and "Populism between fascism and democracy." She has been a visiting professor at the University of Washington, EHESS, Sciences Po, and the Institute of Advanced Studies in Bologna. Recent publications on this topic: "The Populist Twist. The Relationship Between the Leader and the People in Populism" in Pollak/Castiglione (eds.): *Making Present. Theorizing the New Politics of Representation*, University of Chicago Press and "Rosanvallon's concepts of representation and the People and their importance for the understanding of Populism" in Flügel-Martinsen et al. (eds.): *Pierre Rosanvallon's Interdisciplinary Political Thought.* Bielefeld University Press.

Olaf Kaltmeier is Professor of Ibero-American History at the University of Bielefeld. He is director of the CALAS-Maria Sybilla Merian Center for Advanced Latin American Studies in the Humanities and Social Sciences. At Bielefeld University, he is director of the Center for Inter-American Studies (CIAS), coordinator (with Wilfried Raussert) of the BMBF project "The Americas as a space of entanglement," and coordinator of a research axis in the SFB 1288 "Practices of Comparing."

Rüdiger Kunow is Professor Emeritus at the American Studies program at Potsdam University. He has taught at the Universities of Würzburg, Nuremberg, Freiburg, Hanover, and Magdeburg and worked as a Research Fellow at the University of California, Santa Cruz. For various periods of time, he was a visiting professor at the University of Texas at Austin, the State University of New Mexico, Albuquerque, and the State University of New York at Albany. His major research interests and publications focus on cultural constructions of illness and aging, Cultural critique, Transnational American Studies, and the South Asian diaspora in the U.S.

Mirko Petersen is responsible for the recruitment of international students at the Leuphana University of Lüneburg. Before that, he was manager of the BMBF-Project "The Americas as a Space of Entanglements" at the University of Bielefeld. He holds a PhD in history from the University of Bielefeld and a MA degree in European Studies from the University of Constance. His book *Geopoli-*

tische Imaginarien. Diskursive Konstruktionen der Sowjetunion im peronistischen Argentinien (1943-55) came out in 2018 (published by transcript). Among his research interests are Latin American politics, Soviet/Russian-Latin American relations, geopolitics, and populism (in the Americas and Europe).

Heike Raphael-Hernandez is Associate Professor of American Studies at the University of Würzburg, Germany and Adjunct Professor of English at the University of Maryland, University College, Europe. Among her recent publications are *Migrating the Black Body: The African Diaspora and Visual Culture* (with Leigh Raiford, University of Washington Press 2017) and a special issue (with Pia Wiegmink) for the journal *Atlantic Studies*, "German Entanglements in Transatlantic Slavery" 14.4. (Fall 2017), which was republished as a book (Routledge 2018). In addition, she is the editor of *Blackening Europe: The African American Presence* (Routledge 2004) and *AfroAsian Encounters: Culture, History, Politics* (co-edited with Shannon Steen, NYU Press 2006). She is author of *Contemporary African American Women Writers and Ernst Bloch's Principle of Hope* (Edwin Mellen Press 2008) and *Fear, Desire, and the Stranger Next Door: Global South Immigration in American Film* (University of Washington Press 2019), together with Cheryl Finley (Cornell University) and Leigh Raiford.

Claudia Rauhut is research associate and lecturer of Cultural and Social Anthropology at the Institute for Latin American Studies at Freie Universität Berlin. Her current research about Caribbean activism for slavery reparations (founded by the Fritz Thyssen-Foundation) analyzes the redress of transatlantic slavery within the frameworks of reparations for historical injustices. She has published on this topic (i.e. "Mobilizing Transnational Agency for Slavery Reparations: The Case of Jamaica", *The Journal of African American History* 103.1-2, Winter/Spring 2018) as well as on Afro-Cuban religion Santería in the monograph *Santería und ihre Globalisierung in Kuba. Tradition und Innovation in einer afrokuba-*

nischen Religion (2012); and "Las religiones afrocubanas frente a la política migratoria entre Cuba y Estados Unidos", *Foro de Debate sobre Cuba, Iberoamericana* 15.57 (2015). She is co-editor of *Transatlantic Caribbean: Dialogues of People, Practices, Ideas* (2014).

Wilfried Raussert is chair of North American and Inter-American Studies at Bielefeld University and chair of the project "Entangled Americas," a project funded by the Federal Ministry of Research and Education in Germany (2013-2019). He is director of the International Association of Inter-American Studies and co-founder of the Center for Inter-American Studies at Bielefeld University. In 2016, in collaboration with Matti Steinitz, he launched a new international network "The Black Americas/Las négras Américas" which pursues a dialogue between scholars, artists, and activists. He was member of the international committee of the American Studies Association in the U.S. from 2015 until 2018. Among his recent publications are *The Routledge Companion to Inter-American Studies* (2017) and his first book as a photographer, *Art Begins in Streets, Art Lives in Streets* (new urban narratives from the Americas) (2017). He is founder and editor of the online journal *fiar – forum for interamerican research*, the official publication platform of the International Association of Inter-American Studies.

Julia Roth is Professor for American Studies with a focus on Gender Studies at Bielefeld University. Her research interests include postcolonial and gender approaches, critical race studies, intersectionality, and global inequalities. Her current projects focus on gender and citizenship, Caribbean anti-racist feminisms, and hip hop and feminist knowledge production.

Javier Sanjinés is Professor of Latin American Literature and Cultural Studies in the Department of Romance Languages and Literatures at the University of Michigan. He holds a doctoral degree from the University of Minnesota and is currently visiting professor in the History Program at Universidad Andina "Simón Bolívar," in Quito,

Ecuador. He is the author of *Estética y Carnaval. Ensayos de Sociología de la Cultura* (Altiplano, 1984); *Literatura contemporánea y grotesco social en Bolivia* (Friedrich Ebert Stiftung, 1992), re-edited by the *Biblioteca del Bicentenario de Bolivia* (2017); *Mestizaje Upside Down. Aesthetic Politics in Modern* Bolivia (University of Pittsburgh Press, 2004); and *Embers of the Past. Essays in Times of Decolonization* (Duke University Press, 2013). He has published widely on Bolivian cultural issues.

Ulrike Schmieder is a researcher in Latin American Sciences and History, who obtained her PhD at the University of Leipzig and her second doctoral thesis (habilitation) at the University of Cologne. She worked on a research project on Cuba and Martinique in the post-emancipation period. Now she is researcher and lecturer on Iberian, Latin American, and Caribbean History and coordinator of the interdisciplinary Centre for Atlantic and Global Studies and the master's degree Atlantic Studies in History, Culture and Society at the University of Hanover. Her current research project is "Memories of Atlantic Slavery. France and Spain, the French Caribbean and Cuba in Comparison and in the Context of Global Debates on the Remembrance of the Slave Trade and Slavery."

INTER-AMERICAN STUDIES
Cultures – Societies – History

ESTUDIOS INTERAMERICANOS
Culturas – Sociedades – Historia

This interdisciplinary series examines national and transnational issues in the cultures, societies, and histories of the Americas. It creates a forum for a critical academic dialogue between North and South, promoting an inter-American paradigm that shifts the scholarly focus from methodological nationalism to the wider context of the Western Hemisphere.

Vol. 1
Raab, Josef, Sebastian Thies, and Daniela Noll-Opitz, eds. *Screening the Americas: Narration of Nation in Documentary Film / Proyectando las Américas: Narración de la nación en el cine documental.* 2011. 470 pp.

WVT Wissenschaftlicher Verlag Trier	ISBN 978-3-86821-331-7	€ 29,50
Bilingual Press / Editorial Bilingüe	ISBN 978-1-931010-83-2	$ 29.50

Vol. 2
Raussert, Wilfried, and Michelle Habell-Pallán, eds. *Cornbread and Cuchifritos: Ethnic Identity Politics, Transnationalization, and Transculturation in American Urban Popular Music.* 2011. 292 pp.

WVT Wissenschaftlicher Verlag Trier	ISBN 978-3-86821-265-5	€ 29,50
Bilingual Press / Editorial Bilingüe	ISBN 978- 1-931010-80-1	$ 29.50

Vol. 3
Butler, Martin, Jens Martin Gurr, and Olaf Kaltmeier, eds. *EthniCities: Metropolitan Cultures and Ethnic Identities in the Americas.* 2011. 268 pp.

WVT Wissenschaftlicher Verlag Trier	ISBN 978-3-86821-310-2	€ 29,50
Bilingual Press / Editorial Bilingüe	ISBN 978-1-931010-81-8	$ 29.50

Vol. 4
Gurr, Jens Martin, and Wilfried Raussert, eds. *Cityscapes in the Americas and Beyond: Representations of Urban Complexity in Literature and Film.* 2011. 300 pp.

WVT Wissenschaftlicher Verlag Trier	ISBN 978-3-86821-324-9	€ 29,50
Bilingual Press / Editorial Bilingüe	ISBN 978-1-931010-82-5	$ 29.50

Vol. 5
Kirschner, Luz Angélica, ed. *Expanding* Latinidad*: An Inter-American Perspective.*
2012. 292 pp.

| WVT Wissenschaftlicher Verlag Trier | ISBN 978-3-86821-309-6 | € 29,50 |
| Bilingual Press / Editorial Bilingüe | ISBN 978-1-931010-84-9 | $ 29.50 |

Vol. 6
Raussert, Wilfried, and Graciela Martínez-Zalce, eds. *(Re)Discovering 'America': Road Movies and Other Travel Narratives in North America / (Re)Descubriendo 'América': Road movie y otras narrativas de viaje en América del Norte.* 2012. 252 pp.

| WVT Wissenschaftlicher Verlag Trier | ISBN 978-3-86821-384-3 | € 29,50 |
| Bilingual Press / Editorial Bilingüe | ISBN 978-1-931010-91-7 | $ 29.50 |

Vol. 7
Kaltmeier, Olaf, ed. *Transnational Americas: Envisioning Inter-American Area Studies in Globalization Processes.* 2013. 278 pp.

| WVT Wissenschaftlicher Verlag Trier | ISBN 978-3-86821-415-4 | € 29,50 |
| Bilingual Press / Editorial Bilingüe | ISBN 978-1-931010-92-4 | $ 29.50 |

Vol. 8
Raab, Josef, and Alexander Greiffenstern, eds. *Interculturalism in North America: Canada, the United States, Mexico, and Beyond.* 2013. 312 pp.

| WVT Wissenschaftlicher Verlag Trier | ISBN 978-3-86821-460-4 | € 29,50 |
| Bilingual Press / Editorial Bilingüe | ISBN 978-1-931010-99-3 | $ 29.50 |

Vol. 9
Raab, Josef, ed. *New World Colors: Ethnicity, Belonging, and Difference in the Americas.* 2014. 418 pp.

| WVT Wissenschaftlicher Verlag Trier | ISBN 978-3-86821-461-1 | € 29,50 |
| Bilingual Press / Editorial Bilingüe | ISBN 978-1-939743-00-8 | $ 39.50 |

Vol. 10
Roth, Julia. *Occidental Readings, Decolonial Practices: A Selection on Gender, Genre, and Coloniality in the Americas.* 2014. 284 pp.

| WVT Wissenschaftlicher Verlag Trier | ISBN 978-3-86821-446-8 | € 26,50 |
| Bilingual Press / Editorial Bilingüe | ISBN 978-1-939743-07-7 | $ 32.50 |

Vol. 11
Thies, Sebastian, Gabriele Pisarz-Ramirez, and Luzelena Gutiérrez de Velasco, eds. *Of Fatherlands and Motherlands: Gender and Nation in the Americas / De Patrias y Matrias: Género y nación en las Américas.* 2015. 344 pp.

| WVT Wissenschaftlicher Verlag Trier | ISBN 978-3-86821-528-1 | € 29,50 |
| Bilingual Press / Editorial Bilingüe | ISBN 978-1-939743-08-4 | $ 39.50 |

Vol. 12

Fuchs, Rebecca. *Caribbeanness as a Global Phenomenon: Junot Díaz, Edwidge Danticat, and Cristina García.* 2014. 298 pp.

WVT Wissenschaftlicher Verlag Trier	ISBN 978-3-86821-533-5	€ 26,50
Bilingual Press / Editorial Bilingüe	ISBN 978-1-939743-09-1	$ 32.50

Vol. 13

Andres, Julia. *¡Cuéntame algo! – Chicana Narrative Beyond the Borderlands.* 2015. 202 pp.

WVT Wissenschaftlicher Verlag Trier	ISBN 978-3-86821-569-4	€ 25,00
Bilingual Press / Editorial Bilingüe	ISBN 978-1-939743-11-4	$ 28.50

Vol. 14

Hertlein, Saskia. *Tales of Transformation: Emerging Adulthood, Migration, and Ethnicity in Contemporary American Literature.* 2014. 228 pp.

WVT Wissenschaftlicher Verlag Trier	ISBN 978-3-86821-570-0	€ 25,00
Bilingual Press / Editorial Bilingüe	ISBN 978-1-939743-10-7	$ 31.50

Vol. 15

Raab, Josef, and Saskia Hertlein, eds. *Spaces – Communities – Discourses: Charting Identity and Belonging in the Americas.* 2016. 382 pp.

WVT Wissenschaftlicher Verlag Trier	ISBN 978-3-86821-590-8	€ 29,50
Bilingual Press / Editorial Bilingüe	ISBN 978-1-939743-13-8	$ 39.50

Vol. 16

Mehring, Frank, ed. *The Mexico Diary: Winold Reiss between Vogue Mexico and Harlem Renaissance. An Illustrated Trilingual Edition with Commentary and Musical Interpretation* (includes color plates and audio CD). 2016. 244 pp.

WVT Wissenschaftlicher Verlag Trier	ISBN 978-3-86821-594-6	€ 29,50
Bilingual Press / Editorial Bilingüe	ISBN 978-1-939743-14-5	$ 39.50

Vol. 17

Raussert, Wilfried, Brian Rozema, Yolanda Campos, and Marius Littschwager, eds. *Key Tropes in Inter-American Studies: Perspectives from the* forum for inter-american research (fiar). 2015. 374 pp.

WVT Wissenschaftlicher Verlag Trier	ISBN 978-3-86821-627-1	€ 29,50
Bilingual Press / Editorial Bilingüe	ISBN 978-1-939743-16-9	$ 39.50

Vol. 19

Rehm, Lukas, Jochen Kemner, and Olaf Kaltmeier, eds. *Politics of Entanglement in the Americas: Connecting Transnational Flows and Local Perspectives.* 2017. 226 pp.

WVT Wissenschaftlicher Verlag Trier	ISBN 978-3-86821-675-2	€ 27,50
Bilingual Press / Editorial Bilingüe	ISBN 978-1-939743-17-6	$ 32.50

Vol. 20
Britt Arredondo, Christopher. *Imperial Idiocy: A Reflection on Forced Displacement in the Americas.* 2017. 194 pp.

WVT Wissenschaftlicher Verlag Trier	ISBN 978-3-86821-706-3	€ 26,50
Bilingual Press / Editorial Bilingüe	ISBN 978-1-939743-20-6	$ 30.00

Vol. 21
Schemien, Alexia. *Of Virgins, Curanderas, and Wrestler Saints: Un/Doing Religion in Contemporary Mexican American Literature.* 2018. 218 pp.

WVT Wissenschaftlicher Verlag Trier	ISBN 978-3-86821-724-7	€ 27,50
Bilingual Press / Editorial Bilingüe	ISBN 978-1-939743-22-0	$ 32.50

Vol. 22
Fulger, Maria Diana. *The Cuban Post-Socialist Exotic: Contemporary U.S. American Travel Narratives about Cuba.* 2020. 266 pp.

WVT Wissenschaftlicher Verlag Trier	ISBN 978-3-86821-769-8	€ 32,50
Bilingual Press / Editorial Bilingüe	ISBN 978-1-939743-27-5	$ 36.00

Vol. 24
Kaltmeier, Olaf, Mirko Petersen, Wilfried Raussert, and Julia Roth, eds. *Cherishing the Past, Envisioning the Future. Entangled Practises of Heritage and Utopia in the Americas.* 2021. 176 pp.

WVT Wissenschaftlicher Verlag Trier	ISBN 978-3-86821-804-6	€ 23,50
UNO University of New Orleans Press	ISBN 978-1-60801-206-0	$ 27.50

Vol. 26
Raussert, Wilfried. *'What's Going On': How Music Shapes the Social.* 2021. 224 pp.

WVT Wissenschaftlicher Verlag Trier	ISBN 978-3-86821-811-4	€ 28,50
UNO University of New Orleans Press	ISBN 978-1-60801-199-5	$ 34.00

Vol. 27
Frank-Job, Barbara. *Immigration as a Process: Temporality Concepts in Blogs of Latin American Immigrants to Québec.* 2021. 138 pp.

WVT Wissenschaftlicher Verlag Trier	ISBN 978-3-86821-820-6	€ 20,00
UNO University of New Orleans Press	ISBN 978-1-60801-215-2	$ 24.00

Vol. 28
Roth, Julia. *Can Feminism Trump Populism? Right-Wing Trends and Intersectional Contestations in the Americas.* 2021. 166 pp.

WVT Wissenschaftlicher Verlag Trier	ISBN 978-3-86821-821-3	€ 23,00
UNO University of New Orleans Press	ISBN 978-1-60801-205-3	$ 26.00

Vol. 30

Buitrago Valencia, Clara. *Missionaries: Migrants or Expatriates? Guatemalan Pentecostal Leaders in Los Angeles.* 2021. 236 pp.

| WVT Wissenschaftlicher Verlag Trier | ISBN 978-3-86821-818-3 | € 28,50 |
| UNO University of New Orleans Press | ISBN 978-1-60801-210-7 | $ 34.50 |

Vol. 31

Schwabe, Nicole. *De-Centering History Education: Creating Knowledge of Global Entanglements.* 2021. 92 pp.

| WVT Wissenschaftlicher Verlag Trier | ISBN 978-3-86821-828-2 | € 18,00 |
| UNO University of New Orleans Press | ISBN 978-1-60801-214-5 | $ 21.00 |

Vol. 32

Manke, Albert. *Coping with Discrimination and Exclusion. Experiences of Free Chinese Migrants in the Americas in a Transregional and Diachronic Perspective.* 2021. 162 pp.

| WVT Wissenschaftlicher Verlag Trier | ISBN 978-3-86821-829-9 | € 23,00 |
| UNO University of New Orleans Press | ISBN 978-1-60801-207-7 | $ 27.00 |

Vol. 33

Rohland, Eleonora. *Entangled Histories and the Environment? Socio-Environmental Transformations in the Caribbean, 1492-1800.* 2021. 92 pp.

| WVT Wissenschaftlicher Verlag Trier | ISBN 978-3-86821-833-6 | € 18,00 |
| UNO University of New Orleans Press | ISBN 978-1-60801-208-4 | $ 21.00 |

Vol. 34

Kaltmeier, Olaf. *National Parks from North to South. An Entangled History of Conservation and Colonization in Argentina.* 2021. 210 pp.

| WVT Wissenschaftlicher Verlag Trier | ISBN 978-3-86821-834-3 | € 27,50 |
| UNO University of New Orleans Press | ISBN 978-1-60801-204-6 | $ 32.50 |

Vol. 35

Raussert, Wilfried. *Off the Grid. Art Practices and Public Space.* 2021. 232 pp.

| WVT Wissenschaftlicher Verlag Trier | ISBN 978-3-86821-835-0 | € 29,50 |
| UNO University of New Orleans Press | ISBN 978-1-60801-213-8 | $ 34.50 |

Vol. 36

Ravasio, Paola. *This Train Is Not Bound to Glory. A Study of Literary Trainscapes.* 2021. 114 pp.

| WVT Wissenschaftlicher Verlag Trier | ISBN 978-3-86821-836-7 | € 18,00 |
| UNO University of New Orleans Press | ISBN 978-1-60801-216-9 | $ 21.00 |

Vol. 37
Schäfer, Heinrich Wilhelm. *Protestant 'Sects' and the Spirit of (Anti-)Imperialism. Religious Entanglements in the Americas.* 2021. 242 pp.

WVT Wissenschaftlicher Verlag Trier	ISBN 978-3-86821-855-9	€ 29,50
UNO University of New Orleans Press	ISBN 978-1-60801-209-1	$ 34.50